READING *the* SACRED TEXT

☙

What the Torah Tells Us

AARON LICHTENSTEIN

URIM PUBLICATIONS
Jerusalem • New York

Typeset by Ariel Walden

Printed in USA

First Edition

ISBN 978-965-524-164-8

Urim Publications, P.O. Box 5 2 2 8 7
Jerusalem 9 1 5 2 1 0 2 Israel

www.UrimPublications.com

Library of Congress Cataloging-in-Publication Data

Lichtenstein, Aaron, author.
Reading the sacred text : what the Torah tells us / Aaron Lichtenstein.
    pages cm
ISBN 978-965-524-164-8 (hardback)
1. Bible. Old Testament—Hermeneutics. 2. Bible. Old Testament—
Criticism, interpretation, etc., Jewish. I. Title.
BS1186.L53 2015
222'.106—dc23   2015017757

Contents

Preface

UNDERSTANDING THE SACRED TEXT has been a wonderful yet illusive challenge through the ages. In the pages that follow, we seek this understanding by way of a serious reading, based on the proposition that the Torah says what it means and means what it says. Still, this proposition has been a subject of discussion for many years. For example, from the time of the Talmud we have this statement by R. Cahana: "I had finished the Talmud by the time I was eighteen years old, but did not realize until now that a scriptural verse never loses its plain meaning" (*Sabbath* 63).

During the medieval period we have Rashbam concluding a paragraph about interpretation with this comment: "Even Rashi, who is my mother's father and who enlightens our far-flung exile with his commentary on Torah, the Prophets, and the Writings, took care to explain the sentence in its simple meaning (*peshuto shel mikra*) as well. Furthermore, I, Samuel ben Meir, as a relative, argued with him personally, so that he admitted to me that if he had the time he would feel obligated to compose an additional commentary which would reflect the ongoing plain readings" (Rashbam, Genesis 37).

In our own day, we have the forty years of publications by Rabbi Yehuda Cooperman, the dean of Jerusalem's Michlala College for Women, which treat "the sanctity of the simple meaning of the biblical verse."

What our present volume hopes to accomplish is to encourage a reading of the Written Torah which is honest, thoughtful, and secure. What we offer in the pages that follow is an example of what this can accomplish for a reader of the Five Books of Moses. And indeed, we stress that we have before us five books, a division which is basic to their comprehension as literary units. Such a view is explained by Ramban at the end of the Book of Genesis and beginning of the Book of Exodus: "Scripture has concluded its Book of Genesis, which is devoted to the creation of the world and all its creatures ... At the conclusion of this book on creation starts another book which treats the events resulting from the earlier happenings, so that the Book of Exodus concentrates on the first exile, which had been foreordained, and on the redemption from it ... For although these are two books, their narratives are connected by means of the events which follow one another."

Our interpretations too are based on in-context readings which recognize the individual book as the appropriate full context, as each of the five books has its beginning, its end, its purpose, and its accompanying themes.

Our Jewish religious laws and traditional practice, the Halacha, may be viewed as being controlled by the Oral Law; that is, by the Oral Torah instead of the Written Torah.

Today's reader of the Written Torah will simultaneously be aware of the varied disciplines that touch on the Hebrew Bible, such as the archeological, the historical, the linguistic, the national political, the critical, and the dismissive. Even such an awareness does not preclude a return to simply reading the naked text, which is never a simplistic exercise if only because there is Divinity in it, and starts with, "In the beginning God created heaven and earth." Still, the text is intended for a human reader, who must muster all the wisdom and profundity which a mere human is capable of. For in the broadest terms, the Sacred Text is about the relationship between God and mankind.

We turn to our reading in the hope that we are not distracted or dissuaded by a prior ideological commitment. We can be reassured when we study how the Torah says what it means. We turn avidly to the discovery of our own understanding. Presented here are the fruits of our compulsion to know. After all, when we read, "And God said to Moses," we long to hear an echo of the voice of God in the words.　　　　　　　　　　　　　　　　　　—Aaron Lichtenstein

Jerusalem, 2015 / 5775

Part I

Understanding the Book of Genesis

THE TORAH PRESENTS US with three perspectives on creation. The first runs from, "In the beginning God created heaven and earth," through chapter two, verse three: "God blessed the seventh day and sanctified it, for then He rested from all His work which God had done in creation." The next verse introduces a second perspective: "These are the accounts of heaven and earth when created, from the day on which the Lord God made earth and heaven." This verse begins with heaven and earth but ends with earth and heaven, as indeed the first perspective deals primarily with the heavens, while the newly introduced view deals with the scene on earth and centers on mankind. In the first view mankind occupied but one-half a day in a formal seven-day structure, while in the second view mankind is center stage: Without man there would be no need for the rain and vegetation (2:5); all the waters of the world come in service to men's habitation in Eden (2:10); the animals are created only because man needs company (verse 18). While the first view devotes but three sentences to the human, the second view (ending at 4:36) devotes some seventy verses to the emergence of mankind and early human beings.

The first account consistently uses "Elohim" ("God," in most English translations) as the Divine name, while the second account adds the Tetragrammaton, the four-letter proper Divine name ("the Lord," in the common translation), so that the second account uses the combined "the Lord God." Accordingly, the account that treats the human personality invites an added, more personal, aspect of Divinity. The first quoted speech that pronounces the Lord alone belongs to Eve, "I have acquired a man with the Lord," with feelings of gratitude at the birth of Cain (4:1). However, when the Serpent and Eve discuss the forbidden fruit, the formal, universal title, God, is used. And Eve herself, saddened when naming the newborn Seth "as a replacement for Abel, for Cain has murdered him," also reverts to the formal title, "God."

After eating the forbidden fruit, Adam was driven from Eden, and the Lord God "stationed the Cherubim holding a double-edged sword to guard the approach to the Tree of Life" (3:24). A reader may want to interpret figuratively this Divine act preventing Adam's return to Eden. However, ancient texts with a likely memory of this incident, portray the Cherubim as a giant demon whom the hero Gilgamesh attacks so as to enter the Land of the Living with its forest of cedar, and like the builders of the Tower of Babel, to make a name for himself. (See "Gilgamesh" in *Ancient Near Eastern Texts* by James Pritchard.)

Cain's murder of his brother also seems to be remembered in pagan folklore, dating from about the time of the Tower of Babel until Abraham. For example, see in Pritchard, "The dispute between the shepherd-god and the farmer-god," where a strained denial of a fratricide is offered. That Cain's killing Abel remained a matter of concern for generations can be surmised from studying the names of the Seth family. Over half of Seth's named descendants repeat or echo the names of prior persons in the accursed Cain family, as if in a global effort to redeem or fix the curse of Cain through renaming, perhaps reliving. Thus the names Cain, Enoch, Irad, Mehujael, Methusael, Lemech, and again Tubal-Cain, reappear in the geneology of Seth (chapter 5), as Cainan, Enoch, Iarad, Methuselah, Mehalalel, and Lemech. In each case the Seth name appears in a later generation than in the Cain family. Even Noah's naming is expressed in the hope that the newborn boy will be a consolation in redeeming the earth from the curse of Cain, ten generations earlier.

The second account of creation deals not only with the original humans but addresses also the present human reader. Thus, when

Adam marries Eve, one reads, "Therefore does a man leave his father and mother to cleave to his wife, so that they become one body" (2:24). Still, this explanation for the attraction of man and woman is problematic in that Adam's wife-taking did not involve dropping the competing tug of parents, for he had none. Perhaps the point is that since marriage is described as coming earlier – before parenthood – in the ordered sequence of creation, marriage remains a deeper instinct in human consciousness until the present day.

The reader will also note here the initiation of clothing, of making a living, of man versus woman psychology, of cities, music, and mechanics, which remain staples of today's culture.

Chapter five introduces a third perspective of creation: "This is the book of the story of mankind, from the day that God created man – in the fashion of God did He make him. Male and female did He make them; He blessed them and proclaimed them mankind on the very day they were created. Then Adam lived 130 years and became a father in his own likeness...." What follows is a list with ten generations, using identical formulaic language for each father and son. This third creation account projects not the individual, but the ongoing human race, moving methodically from father to son. This third view is termed a book, and indeed it records information over time, giving the birth and death years for each successive party. The term "book" also points to the Book of Genesis as a whole, whose main characters are the patriarchs starting with Abraham, so that the genealogy listing helps place the elaborate patriarchal story in a time frame tied to the Beginning.

The name for Divinity here is again Elohim, God, just as it was in the first account, as this third account too is more global than personal.

Although the Torah presents creation from three successive perspectives, the information in an earlier account is often carried over into the next account. An example of this is the reason why humans die, which is explained in the second account, but which is given prominence in the third. Why everybody must die is the most poignant fact in the second. The third account punctuates this lesson by ending each person's mention with "and he died," repeating the dread fact of human mortality. The case of Enoch is the exception that underscores the rule: "Enoch walked with god, then he disappeared, because God had taken him" (5:24), omitting the expected death. That the phrase "and he died" does not appear in the next ten-generation list, from Noah to Abraham in chapter eleven, makes clear that the lesson of human mortality is central to the story of creation. The chapter eleven list closes each life instead with "and he had sons and daughters."

On the other hand, a thematic word, "to begin" (here *huchal*), serves to tie the flood to the creation narrative, as an extension of the Beginning: "They began then to call the Lord by name (4:26). This form of "to begin" appears another half-dozen times, using various Hebrew grammatical forms meaning "to begin," "to be ready to begin," "to wait to restart," "to prompt or induce," in 6:1, 8:10, 8:12, 9:20, 10:8, and 11:6. We do not find this form again until the very end of the book, with Joseph in Egypt, and it does not appear in all of Exodus and Leviticus.

That the flood's destruction is portrayed as an extension of the world's creation – as creation canceled and as creation in reverse – is implied in 6:6: "The Lord was sorry that He had created mankind on earth and He was sad. Said the Lord, 'I shall destroy this mankind I created from off the face of the earth – man, animal, creepers, and birds – for I am sorry that I made them.' But Noah found favor in the eyes of the Lord." The theological perplexity of having a mistake attributed to the Omniscient underscores that the decision to undo is here an extension of the decision to do, and the repetition of the fact that He is their creator in the first place says as much.

We note too, that the more personal Divine name, the Lord, is used in this passage, indicating that the full force of Divine compassion was exercised in arriving at the decision for doom. Along the same lines, we find the personal "the Lord" used when the Divine Judge "goes down to examine the city and the Tower which the sons of man were building" (11:5), before a decision to scatter Babel's builders. In both cases, the compassionate quality of Divinity is expressed, preventing a misreading attributing callousness or anger to the decision for guilt. The point is emphasized further in the empathy suggested by the extreme anthropomorphism of God being sorry and of God going down to check the evidence against the Tower's builders.

Divine mercifulness having been articulated, the flood story itself switches again to the formal universal title, God. As creation in reverse, the flood story features the same universal aspects of Divinity found in the initial creation account, God.

That the world survived the deluge was due in part to the cooperation of man, the righteous Noah, and to God's precise orders on how to build an ark, comprising a reaffirmation of existence. In this new effort, mankind itself – whose evil caused the destruction – is called upon to be an active partner with the Eternal in creation's reformulation. Along the same lines, after Moses smashed the Tablets of the Law when he saw the Golden Calf, he himself was required to hew the second set, upon which God would reinscribe the commandments.

There are numerous parallels in the wording of creation and of creation's reaffirmation during the deluge: The number seven is prominent; the concern for animals; heaven and earth repeatedly; day and night are stressed; the waters and the deep abyss are there; male and female mentioned often; three children for Adam and three for Noah with their wives; the animals respecified as animal, beast, creepers, and birds; food is needed; upper and lower levels in separation; the trees of Eden and the Gopher-tree wood for Noah's ark; creation began with light and the ark has a skylight (*Zohar*); the spirit or wind of God over the waters; Seth's Enoch walked with God and Noah walked with God; the world begins with primordial water only to be destroyed by water; a cunning, aggressive serpent versus a smart, helpful dove; Adam was created when a misty cloud arose, and Noah's rainbow covenant rises in a cloud; Noah's sacrifice prompts a switch to the Divine personal name as did Abel's sacrifice; Cain's sacrifice efforts end in murder and a curse, while Noah's sacrifice brings on a blessing and the law against murder.

Note that it was the Lord who accepted Abel and cursed Cain but that it was the man Noah who, after the flood, was empowered to bless his son Shem and to curse Canaan. We have here an early indication of how the Book of Genesis, which begins with God alone and with God the prime mover, gradually moves to telling the story of human characters and their initiatives, so that by the end of the book, where we are told about the patriarch Jacob's family, there are hardly any Divine initiatives recorded, but instead human initiatives which, however, reflect on and report on the Almighty.

Noah's sacrifice, which represented the worship of all mankind, elicited a Divine resolution for a new, tolerant relationship with the earth: "... I shall never again curse the earth because of Mankind, for men's hearts are inclined toward evil from the start ..." (8:21). Thus, in this new world order, we find Nimrod, and others who follow his example, provoking the Divine by being an aggressive warrior in God's face, but we find no retribution noted for his pride or conquest. And when the first inhabitants of Babylon declare in chapter eleven, "Come now, let us fire bricks ... Come now, let us build a city with a tower whose top touches heaven and let us make a name for ourselves," the Divine response is but a gentle interference: "Come now, let Us go down there and confuse their language, so that one will not understand another's language." God's response mimics the very words of the builders, and has the tone of an amused schoolmaster quipping "boys will be boys."

The rainbow becomes the sign of a Divine promise against there ever being a deluge again. God tells Noah, in part, "When there is a rainbow in a cloud, I shall look upon it as a reminder of the eternal covenant between God and all living things ..." (9:16). The symbolism here probably derives from the first Divine judgmental act after the first act of creation: "God looked at the light and saw that it was good." The rainbow, which is light in its full spectrum, is a reminder of the decision to make a world, and now to see it in a favorable light. The cloud here recalls the creation of man, where the mention of rainclouds is prominent in the second creation narrative. In the imagination of the people in Genesis, God is seen as being in heaven above, so that God would see the rainbow from the top, while people would see it from earth below, with the two ends of the rainbow fashioning a perpetual connection between heaven and earth. By way of the rainbow covenant, God invites Himself to consider the light as still good.

Chapter ten tells us how the families of Noah's three sons, Shem,

Ham, and Japheth, populated the earth, each remaining separate and distinct. Mentioned are some seventy founding fathers, families, states, language groups, or nationalities. Some reappear in Genesis and are recognized in the ongoing narrative, as for example, Sodom and Gomorrah, Egypt, Aram, Babylon, Canaan, Asshur, Gerar, the Philistines, the Hittites, Jebusites, Amorites, Girgashites, and Hivites. All would have been identifiable by the time Moses completed the Torah in Deuteronomy 31: "So it was that Moses finished the writing of the words of this Torah, to the last word." (For the identity of the seventy nations and for the attendant geography, see Aryeh Kaplan, *The Living Torah*.)

Ham's family is granted fifteen verses, which is as much as Shem and Japheth get together, because of the full treatment of Ham's Canaan, with whom the patriarchs must soon share the Holy Land, until such time as "the sins of the Amorite are overabundant," when Israel is to inherit the land.

The family of Noah's favorite son, Shem, is placed last, so that it can be followed by the upcoming Shem-line genealogy directly to Abraham (still named Abram). And Shem is reintroduced here as "the forefather of all the Hebrews." Abraham's father Terach is given a lot of space, so that, in part, Abraham's family, his wife and nephew Lot, can be introduced. Still, God's call to Abraham at the start of chapter twelve is jolting in its suddenness and breathtaking in its scope: "The Lord said to Abram, 'Leave your homeland for the country that I will show you; I shall make you into a great nation and bless you ...'" By contrast, before God spoke to Noah, we read, "Noah found favor in the Lord's eyes ... Noah was the righteous, perfect man of his generation; Noah walked with God." But for Abraham the reader is not so prepared. The suddenness may be due to the assumption that every reader of the Torah would have prior knowledge of Abraham's relationship with the Divine. Or, from the Divine perspective, Abraham was so precious that no formal introduction would do him justice.

Chapter thirteen tells of the dispute over land rights that arose between Abraham's and nephew Lot's shepherds. Abraham steps in to solve the dispute, saying, "But we are like brothers." The word "brother" appears twice and triggers the memory of brothers Cain and Abel in their dispute over land rights, which ended in murder.

Abraham tells Lot to choose part of the land he wishes to reserve for himself, so Abraham would go the other way. "Lot raised up his eyes and saw the whole valley of the Jordan, how fertile it was before the Lord destroyed Sodom and Gomorrah, that it was like a garden of the Lord, like the land of Egypt, as far as Zoar; Lot chose all the Jordan Valley. . . ." The phrase "raise up your eyes and see" appears a dozen times in Genesis, but only in connection with a patriarch or matriarch: Abraham, Isaac, Rebecca, Jacob, Judah's brothers, and Joseph. The expression implies that the sacred text applauds the scene or action, as if to say: He lifted his eyes toward Heaven and complied or understood. The phrase is not found in all Exodus or Leviticus even for Moses or Aaron. That the phrase appears here for Lot as he is about to abandon Abraham to move near the Sodomites, indicates that Lot's blessedness is portrayed the moment before he is stripped of his spiritual brotherhood with Abraham. And at once, the phrase is used for Abraham: "The Lord said to Abraham after Lot left him, 'Raise your eyes and look . . . all the land that you see I shall give you.'" For both Abraham and Lot, the phrase was used here upon viewing sacred soil.

But Abraham does not abandon Lot. When Lot was captured in the war of the four against the five kings, Abraham comes to "his brother's" aid. The account of this war is presented as an excursus, as military history coming from an outside, objective source. The opening, "It came to pass in the days of Amraphel King of Shinar," indicates a new document, comparable to the start of the Esther Scroll, "It came to pass in the days of Achashverosh . . ." And when Abraham comes to the rescue, he is tagged "Abram the Hebrew," a new identification, as if for an unknown person. The designation "Hebrew" is standard when identifying for outsiders and foreigners. Thus, Joseph enters Egypt as a Hebrew slave, the Philistines object to David's Hebrews, and Jonah tells the sailors he is a Hebrew. An outsider's account allows the reader to hear seeming disinterested evaluations of our hero, that he is loyal, fearless, a victorious warrior, generous, an international figure of stature, but totally devoted to God. When Malchizedek, the royal priest of God On High, arrives to celebrate the victory, he receives Abraham's tithe. But when the vanquished King of Sodom invites Abraham to take some of the prize of war, Abraham rebuffs him, lest the Sodomites say they made Abraham rich. And while "God On High" is an approved term for Divinity in the narration, Abraham is careful to add the ineffable, "the Lord God On High," in his oath.

In chapter fifteen, we are introduced to yet another Divine name, "Our Master Divine," in an English approximation. It appears only when a supplicant prays to God. It features here twice as Abraham prays, and again in Deuteronomy 3:23 and 9:26, in prayers by Moses.

When Hagar runs away from Sarah's punishment in chapter sixteen, an angel accosts her: "The angel of the Lord said to her, 'Return to your mistress and submit to her punishment.' The angel of the Lord said to her, 'I will multiply your offspring, they will be too numerous to count.' The angel of the Lord said to her, 'You are pregnant and shall have a son; call him Ishmael for the Lord has heard your pain. But he will be a beast of a man, he will be into everything and everyone will provoke him and he will live in confrontation with everybody.'"

These three speeches to Hagar comprise an anatomy of what was in reality a single complex, ramified statement to Hagar. In effect, the first statement says that Sarah is right, the second statement says that Hagar is right, and the third indicates some middle ground, that Hagar will have Ishmael – whereas Sarah is still barren – but that Ishmael will be a wild man and unworthy of being the next patriarch. (A similar presentation of such a tripartite Divine message occurs in Exodus 33:19.)

The seventeenth chapter represents the book's third Divine covenant. The first was the Rainbow Covenant with Noah, which promised no more deluges. This covenant involved no contributing human participation. The book's second covenant promised the Holy Land to Abraham: "On that day did the Lord set a covenant with Abram saying, 'To your children have I given this land, from the Brook of Egypt to the wide river Euphrates'" (15:18). This second covenant required Abraham's participation in preparing a mystical sacrificial ritual, with God's flaming spirit passing through in agreement. But the third covenant calls for repeated human participation: "This is the covenant which you are to observe between me and you, and your children after you, circumcise for yourselves every male …" (17:10). The Divine's part in the agreement is the promise that Abraham and Sarah will have children, a family, even a nation, and the word "children" appears a half-dozen times in the full agreement. That the promise for children should be signaled by attention to the reproductive organ remains unsaid.

As a prelude to the covenant on circumcision, God tells Abram that henceforth his name will be Abraham, meaning a patriarch to many nations. Sarai's new name is Sarah, or mistress *par excellence*. God is soon to name Isaac and He has already named Ishmael. These Divine namings are striking here, because from the beginning naming was seen as a human prerogative. This intervention is but one of the modes of the Divine's involvement with His favorite family, found throughout the Book of Genesis.

Translators have associated Isaac's name, *Yitzhak*, with laughter, *tzehok*. However, instead of laughter we may be dealing here with exultation, and this seems to be how the word's root is used in the Ugaritic epics, dating to roughly Abraham's times and unearthed in the Lebanon. If so, Genesis 17:17 would read:

> Abraham fell to his face and exulted, saying in his heart, "Shall indeed a hundred-year-old man engender and shall Sarah, a ninety-year-old woman, give birth?" Said Abraham to God, "Would that Ishmael live in Your good favor." Said God, "But Sarah your wife bears you a son and you are to call him Isaac (exultation, joy, celebration, triumph)."
> Genesis 21:6: Sarah said, "God has let me exult; all who hear will celebrate with me … Who would have said of Abraham that Sarah shall nurse children, yet have I borne him a son of old age."

Then, Genesis 26:8, "Avimelech the Philistine king looked out of the window and saw Isaac 'Isaac-ing' with Rebecca his wife," would refer not to Isaac laughing with Rebecca, but to his appropriate matrimonial success.

That Isaac's name signifies something positive like triumph or exultation, seems to be recalled in the misspelling of his name in Amos 7:9, "The high places of Isaac (*Yishak*) will turn desolate."

Spelling the name with an "s" instead of the usual "tz," constitutes a stinging jab at the people of Isaac, who, named for success, are turned in Amos's prophecy of doom into laughing stocks and losers. For *sehok* is the Hebrew root connoting laughter, poking fun, play, sport, and jest; whereas basic *tzehok*, without preposition, expresses openness, unselfconscious exuberance, celebration of glory, and exultation.

After God tells Abraham that he will have Isaac and commands the ritual of circumcision, verse 22 adds, "So He finished speaking to him and God ascended off Abraham." What follows describes how conscientiously Abraham circumcised his household, and verse 22 explains that Abraham had total freedom of action, to obey or disobey, and that it was not the influence of God's presence that propelled his obedience. This mention of Abraham's freedom of choice will apply to the rest of Abraham's career, particularly to the Binding of Isaac years later.

Even in chapter eighteen, there is change in the way Divinity approaches Abraham: "The Lord revealed himself to him ... and he raised up his eyes and saw three men standing before him." It will slowly dawn on the reader, and on Abraham as well, that these three gentlemen are the revelation: That they represent God, that they are perhaps angels, and that their words are God's. This intermediate form of revelation reduces the force of the Divine glory on Abraham. Perhaps this form of revelation permits the Divine to interrelate with His favorite human, while permitting the devotee to respond with the free will, which makes him worthy of God's attention.

When Sarah laughs in disbelief at the gentlemen's promise of her having a son, they tell on her to Abraham. Presumably, Abraham upbraids Sarah, but she answers, "I did not laugh," and he says, "Not so, you did laugh." What the gentlemen accomplished by instigating this domestic dispute was having husband and wife confront each other over their barrenness, and eventually to lovingly reconcile for having a child.

The indeterminateness of this revelation is reflected in the variety of Divine names used. The authoritative narration terms the gentlemen's statements the Lord's, but Abraham, and later Lot, continuously call them "my masters." And when we read in verse twenty-two, "Then the men departed for Sodom, but Abraham remained standing before the Lord; and Abraham stepped forward and said, 'Would You destroy the righteous ones together with the guilty ones?'" Abraham here is addressing the remaining third gentleman, whom he calls "my master," and this is why Abraham can permit himself to question Divinity so audaciously. And this is why only two of the three gentlemen are shown arriving in Sodom. Lot greets them as "my masters," but the narration now terms them angels, men, or the Lord.

Abraham's pleading for Sodom and Gomorrah comes in response to God's informing him that the cities were under indictment. In 18:17, God explains why He must inform Abraham: "'Shall I hide from Abraham what I am about to do, when Abraham is destined to found a great and mighty people, through whom all the peoples of the earth will be blessed?' ... So the Lord informed, 'The shrieking from Sodom and Gomorrah is terrible and their sins are very heavy; I shall go down there to examine the outcry ...'" Still, why would it have been wrong to withhold the impending doom from Abraham? The answer becomes obvious as we read verse 16, "The men took their leave from there and they peered toward Sodom, with Abraham accompanying them, seeing them off." By accompanying his erstwhile guests, now on their way to destroy Sodom, Abraham unwittingly leaves himself open to being accused of cooperating in clearing the Promised Land of its inhabitants so that he could inherit it. Thus, on being made aware of the gentlemen's upcoming mission, Abraham goes to an opposite extreme, arguing on behalf of Sodom. The safety of his nephew Lot is not a factor in Abraham's plea, and it comes as a surprise after the destruction that we read, "So it was that when God destroyed the cities of the valley, God thought of Abraham and extricated Lot from the upheaval" (19:29).

When Isaac is finally born and celebrated, Sarah spots an attitude of unacceptable rivalry in Ishmael and, with Divine concurrence, she has Abraham send Ishmael and Hagar away. Hagar loses her way in the BeerSheva desert and places Ishmael – dying of thirst – under a tree: "She walked away as far as a bow's shot, thinking, 'Let me not watch the boy die,' and she sat by and cried" (21:16). God sends an angel to save them, and the story moves quickly to Ishmael's growing up to be a desert bowman and to his mother's bringing him a wife from Egypt. The ambivalence of the text toward Ishmael is marked repeatedly. That he would grow up to be a shooter of arrows is prefigured in Hagar's crying at a bowshot's distance from him. That mother Hagar, herself an Egyptian, brings him an Egyptian wife, redoubles the gap between the Semite patriarchal family and the Hamite Ishmaelite family. As for Ishmael himself, he is later accorded a place of honor alongside Isaac at the funeral of Abraham; and Ishmael's own passing is warmly eulogized in chapter twenty-five, with mention that he fathered twelve clans – a favorable parallel to Israel's twelve tribes. Still, the mention there of Egypt as adjoining the expansive Ishmaelite territory, adds a sour note, as does the eulogy's last phrase: that the Ishmaelites would descend plague-like upon all their surroundings – this a poisoned variation on the prophetic phrase of the angel in 16:2, that the Ishmaelites would dwell quietly near all their surroundings.

The high point of Abraham's life story is the Binding of Isaac, in chapter 22. Prior to this test, Abraham is pictured in tranquility, having achieved an armistice with the Philistine monarch and living for many years in Philistine lands undisturbed. He is able to pursue the mission of spreading his faith, and introduces yet another form of the Divine name, the Lord God Eternal. God Himself had introduced the previous innovative name, God Almighty, in chapter 17.

Suddenly, the tranquility is shattered when God commands him to sacrifice his beloved son Isaac. The reader is advised this is only a test, but Abraham would have never experienced such a possibility in his relationship to God. The name for Divinity in this test is God, stressing His universality, instead of the Lord, the personal aspect of Divinity with which Abraham was approached. And indeed, a test would call for transcendence, given the impartiality that a test implies.

Abraham was beset not only by fear for his dear son but by a perplexing theological quandary, for God's truth had promised that Isaac would become his spiritual successor. Somehow, traveling to the secret mountain, Abraham was able to overcome these doubts and was able to arrange for the sacrifice in obedience to God's command. Isaac's willingness to be sacrificed, mother Sarah's eventual horror, and the theological implications, are all omitted, because the narrative is single-mindedly portraying the hero Abraham's phenomenal attachment to God. When Abraham, knife in hand, is stopped at the last moment, it becomes the Lord's angel, not God's, who stops him, because – the test being over – Abraham's personal relationship with Divinity reasserts itself.

Just as the section preceding the Binding of Isaac contributes to a full appreciation of Abraham's stature, the section that follows does so as well: "Thereafter it was reported to Abraham, 'Here, Milka too has borne children unto Nahor your brother …'" (22:20). What follows are the names of the eight sons of Milka and four more born to Nahor's concubine, Reuma. These parallels between Abraham with Sarah and Nahor with Milka – and Hagar and Reuma too – respond to a nagging question which undercuts the tremendously heroic portrait of Abraham: Perhaps Abraham was ready to sacrifice Isaac because Isaac was a mere magical child, provided by a Divine miracle to a barren woman and aged man, that Abraham may not have had the natural biological sympathy that accompanies normal engendering. Stories about such magical children were unearthed in ancient Ugaritic and Sumerian legends. The immediate parallel to brother Nahor's birthing drives such a demeaning suspicion from the reader's mind. Although the birth of Nahor's granddaughter Rebecca is mentioned because of her future prominence, the bulk of the Nahor news here provides support for the absolute heroism of Abraham in the Binding of Isaac, and this is why Nahor's news is couched as a report to Abraham.

Indeed, that the birth of Isaac was announced in the context of Abimelekh's abduction of Sarah, makes a similar point: Chapter twenty ends, "Abraham prayed to God and God healed Abimelekh and his wives and maids, so that they gave birth. For the Lord had sealed all the wombs of Abimelekh's household because of Sarah Abraham's wife. Then the Lord took note of Sarah, as He had promised, and the Lord did for Sarah what He had predicted. So Sarah became pregnant and gave birth of a son of Abraham's old age."

It does not take a scoundrel to wonder how come the barren Sarah finally has a child after being taken to the Philistine palace. Indeed, the text invites his question by placing Sarah's name in both the last sentence of the abduction event and in the first sentence of her giving birth. The full narrative repeats over a dozen times that Isaac is Abraham's son. But the benefit that accrues from the fleeting question is that it characterizes Abraham's paternity of Isaac as natural a biological event, as that of a lewd abduction, or as that of Abimelekh's queen and maids having children.

Even the earlier narratives create an atmosphere of sensuality, against any imagined magical birthing: an Egyptian king seeking a pretty woman, Hagar's birthing, Sodom's sensuality, Lot offering the girls to the mob, the drunken Lot fathering Moab and Ben-Ammi, and Abraham's circumcision prior to engendering Isaac.

Abraham's taking another wife, after Sarah's death, also sustains the view of Abraham as being a natural father. In the first place, this even older Abraham has many children with this Keturah, showing him as naturally prolific. Then, he gives gifts to the new offspring – now termed "a concubine's offspring" – and sends them away from "Isaac his son" (25:6).

The Binding of Isaac is the culmination of Abraham's career, and thereafter we are not told of any glorious accomplishment. When Sarah dies and Abraham needs to purchase a burial plot, the locals outsmart him. Abraham had refused the Hittites' gracious offer to inter Sarah in their cemetery, and archeology provides evidence that Hittite burials were replete with pagan rituals. Rather, Abraham wishes to buy the duplex cave at the edge of Ephron's field. Ephron responds by saying he gives it to him free, and throws in the whole field too. Abraham goes along and says he is willing to buy the whole field as well. Ephron replies, "Let us not quibble over land worth a mere 400 shekel, bury your dead" (25:15). Abraham pays. The ancient Hittite Law Code legislates prices for fields at two shekel for a one-acre field and one shekel if the field is far from town. Abraham was interested only in the cave, but Ephron's sales pitch moved from cave, to field, to land, winning him a wildly overpriced sale. The respectful Hittite leaders in attendance do not protest and the bereaved husband is cheated.

However, the narration lets loose with a warm applause over this deal: Abraham had just made the first purchase in the Promised Land for the Chosen People, and one cannot overpay acquiring sacred national land.

After burying Sarah, Abraham sends his servant, his household manager, to bring a wife for Isaac from Aram, the family birthplace. The servant, or slave, who remains nameless, leads a caravan of camels bearing gifts to Aram, and then prays, "... I am here at the spring while the city's daughters are out fetching water. Let the girl to whom I say, 'Lower your flask so I may drink,' who answers, 'Drink and to your camels also will I give water,' be the girl whom You designate for Your servant Isaac." The very first girl approached gives the right answer, and the servant hands her the jewelry he had ready to make the match.

It turns out that Abraham's servant is as able a salesman as Ephron the Hittite, and even knows when it is right to lie for the cause. When he realizes that this girl happens to be Rebecca, the servant lies and tells them that Abraham sent him to find a girl from the family for Isaac, whereas in truth Abraham's orders only were, "Do not pick a wife for my son from the Canaanite daughters among whom I live, but go to my country of birth to pick a wife for my son Isaac."

This rejection of the Canaanites essentially goes back to Noah's curse, but it also ties in with the prior event, in which the local folk seem insensitive to Ephron's sharp business practices against "a prince of God in our midst."

Taking advantage of this appearance of a family member, the servant – in a lengthy retelling of everything – convinces Rebecca's family that it was no coincidence, but God's miracle and that this match was made in heaven.

His lengthy speech is full of changes and omissions that support his version of Abraham's words. The text has him giving the girl the jewelry first to discover only later that she is family, but the servant's retelling reverses the order. Abraham had said that Isaac must never move to Aram – and Abraham had just purchased a field in the Promised Land – but the servant omits this refusal to live in Aram, as it might be taken as an insult to the Aramean family. Abraham's order read absolutely no Canaanite wife, but the servant changes it to no Canaanite wife unless the family offers no bride.

While the servant certainly was lying about Abraham's precise command, the reader realizes that his basic sales pitch is correct, that whatever happened to him in Aram was the work of God. In the first place, his master had promised that "God in heaven … shall send His angel before you so you can bring Isaac a wife from there." Secondly, Rebecca's name appeared as soon as Isaac was unbound, in 22:23, and when she is identified again in Aram, her relationship to Abraham's family is rendered using the very same terminology, hinting that the match was preordained. And indeed, when Rebecca arrives on camelback, "Isaac lifts up his eyes and sees," and "Rebecca lifts up her eyes and sees," assuring us that this is a marriage made in heaven.

That Rebecca has the character needed for the emerging patriarchal family was already indicated when she drew the water "hurriedly," an action attributed to her three times. Only Abraham was presented acting with such alacrity, when he prepared the meal for his three guests, with "hurrying" mentioned three times.

On returning, the servant does not give his report to his master Abraham but to the groom, Isaac. Isaac comes to love Rebecca, "so that Isaac was consoled on the loss of his mother." The last remark forms yet another link between the two adjoining events, the purchase of a gravesite for Sarah and the finding of a wife for Isaac.

Rebecca, like Sarah before her, is barren. But Sarah's barrenness was told over many chapters, while Rebecca's is noted and resolved in one brief sentence, after prayers. This pattern of barrenness persists into the third patriarchal generation, with Rachel's anguished longing for a child. We have here a parallel between God blessing humankind at creation with the ability to reproduce and God's ongoing involvement in this regard with His favorite family. And after all, at the first birth in history, Eve had announced, "I have made a person together with the Lord."

Also like Eve, Rebecca produces two warring lads, one a shepherd and the other "a man of the field" and hunter. In the end, it would take steady appeasement to prevent a repeat of fratricide – this reversal pointing to perhaps a general respite from such murder. In the meantime, the brothers engage in business of their own, this time no one is cheating, and the firstborn sells his birth-right for a meal of lentils, a sale which Esau, the firstborn, will regret in tears.

There comes yet another hunger in the land and Isaac moves to Philistine territory, and for the third time a matriarch is threatened with abduction by the ruler. These repeated threats project Divine involvement in keeping the patriarchal family intact. But in this third such incident, it is the reader who expects Divine interven-tion in a story that is well known, whereas here the text describes no miracle, only broad assurance of God's protection. Here we have another instance of how the Book of Genesis begins with Divinity at center of the action, but gradually shifts the focus to human initiatives, leaving to the attentive reader, and to the char-acters, the appreciation of Divinity's lasting influence.

The end of chapter 26 returns to the brothers' tale. This alter-nating between different scenes is found regularly in the Genesis narrative to indicate either simultaneousness or overlap. For a full appreciation of events, the reader is asked to keep two or more strands in mind, which results in a complex and ramified perspec-tive – especially needed because of the continual Divine perspec-tive present.

Esau is the brother treated here, when he takes two Hittite wives who, as expected, are a vexation for Isaac and Rebecca. Still, neither here nor later is Esau ever branded evil in an authorita-tive way, the final such branding in Genesis occurring with the evil Sodomites. But Esau's troublesome marriages prepared us for what follows: whether Esau or Jacob merits their father's blessing.

There is a good deal of repetition in the telling of this event in chapter 27. But just as in the seeming repetition in the servant's Aram speech, there are important variations in the repeats. Father Isaac said to Esau, "so that my soul will bless you before I die," but Rebecca repeats it for Jacob, "will bless you before the Lord before I die." That is, she is aghast at her husband's mistake because it would also be sacrilege. And early on Rebecca had demonstrated her independence and her independent access to the Divine word, when she went to inquire about the contentious twins in her womb. Now she decks out Jacob like Esau and sends him in to her near-blind husband for his blessing. Jacob enters and repeats,

"Let your soul bless me," but respectfully omits "before you die." When Esau belatedly arrives for the blessing, he too respectfully omits mention of the father's death.

Isaac inspects Jacob by touch, and says, "The voice is the voice of Jacob, and the hands (draped in shearling) are the hands of Esau." When Jacob kisses his father, he responds, "See, the odor of my son is like the fragrance of a blessed field ..." The incongruity of seeing a smell alerts us to the fact that Isaac is engaged here using all five senses. He tastes the food and wine, he hears the voice, he touches the hands, and he smells the aroma. As for sight, since Isaac was described as near-blind, the sense of sight is combined with another sense, with smell, conveying how all the human senses were active when Isaac bestowed his blessing on Jacob.

On learning that Jacob has stolen his blessing, Esau blurts out, "He was named Jacob [from the Hebrew for 'heel'] so he has tripped me up twice, he took my birthright and now he has taken my blessing." This utterance of the moaning Esau serves to soften the severity of Jacob's lie in misrepresenting himself to his father, for Jacob had acquired the primogeniture. And while Esau had said, "I am your son, your firstborn, Esau," Jacob's misarrangement of the words could convey, "It is verily I who am Esau as firstborn." Further, after Esau's squandering of the birthright, only Esau continued to call himself the firstborn, while the narration terms him the elder or senior brother, and Jacob the younger or junior brother.

Rebecca's machinations on behalf of her dear Jacob do not mean that she disowns Esau. On the contrary, her motherliness for both is retained when she tells Jacob to run away to Aram in face of Esau's fury and adds, "... why should I lose the both of you in one day?" Neither does Esau drop his respect for his mother, and when he hears that Jacob is to marry a girl with his mother's pedigree, he is prompted to marry a girl of equal lineage, namely, "Mahalath daughter of Ishmael, son of Abraham, and sister to Nevayoth." The mention of sister to Nevayoth is instructive because Nevayoth was listed as the firstborn and the possessor of the very status that Esau was jealously trying to reclaim.

But Jacob is pained over the loss of a brother's friendship. The first words he utters on greeting some Aramean strangers are "my brothers," and the word "brother" appears over a half-dozen times upon Jacob's arrival in Aram, and is still prominent twenty years later when on his belated departure he terms his dinner guests "brothers" (31:54).

On his trip to Aram, Jacob spends a last night within the Holy Land at "the place," a term used three times in a single verse and ten times in all, six times here and four more when Jacob returns to "the place" twenty years later. This thematic word is given a double meaning. In his sleep at "the place," Jacob is granted a revelation, with God promising to bequeath to him the ground on which he is asleep. On awakening, an enraptured Jacob names "the place" the House of God, Bethel, but in the revelation "the place" was emblematic of the entire Promised Land, which he is to inherit. The spiritual insignificance of outside locations is indicated by Jacob's departure for "Eastern lands," now omitting the destination as Haran in Aram.

Jacob's giving a name to Bethel prefigures his mastery of the land he is about to leave. His predecessors Abraham and Isaac were also pictured giving names to Canaanite spots, such as BeerSheva, Rechovoth, and Yireh. Later, as soon as Jacob returns as close as Transjordan, he names Mahanayim and Penuel. But during a twenty-year sojourn in Aram he gives no names, for the land is not his. Even Joseph as viceroy in Egypt is not shown naming places – a stranger in a strange land.

The shepherds at a well near Haran point out to Jacob that the shepherdess approaching is Rachel, his mother's niece. Jacob is so moved by her propitious coming that he singlehandedly rolls the massive stone off of the well and proceeds to re-enact the betrothal scene that took place between Abraham's servant and Rebecca his mother. "His mother" is stressed three times in a single verse. Whereas at his mother's betrothal it was she, the future bride, who demonstrated her capability of servicing both the servant and his animals with water, in Jacob's case it was left to the groom to service the bride and her animals. He drew water for the sheep but as for serving Rachel – who was clueless about what was happening – Jacob substituted a kiss: Our text uses the same consonantal letters for "he gave to drink" and for "he gave a kiss," VYShK.

Jacob is soon welcomed into the home of Rachel's father, Laban.

The innocent Jacob tells Laban everything – that he is on the run from Esau and that he has been sent to fetch a wife. Laban begins at once to take advantage of him. When the penniless Jacob offers to work a seven-year cycle for the hand of the lovely Rachel, Laban agrees, but then slips in Leah instead on the wedding night. Laban's excuse, "We do not do this in our country, to give away or put the younger girl before the firstborn" (29:26). The uncalled for use of "firstborn" turns Laban's explanation into a nasty jab at Jacob: The two sisters had been introduced as "Leah the elder and Rachel the younger," but by substituting "the firstborn" Laban is telling Jacob that if he is a runaway in Haran it is because he put himself before the firstborn Esau, and that the Arameans are an honest people who don't engage in such underhanded conduct.

With blatant insensitivity, Laban goes on to refer to his two daughters as "this one and that one," while for Jacob it is a matter of getting the woman he loves. Jacob commits himself to working another seven years for Rachel, "He took Rachel also and he loved Rachel also more than Leah." This jagged verse reflects the precarious emotional state of Jacob's marriages to the sisters, two dear sisters who will compete for Jacob's affection. Their competition is spelled out when they choose names for their respective sons. For example, on the birth of Levi, "Now my husband will stick to me, for I have given him three sons." And on the birth of Naphtali, "I am engaged in an Almighty wrestling match with my sister, and have won." The envy between the sisters is passed on to their separate children in early childhood, and this becomes the early psychological cause for the splintering of Jacob's sons, ultimately leading to the brothers selling Joseph into slavery. This contagion is illustrated in the first appearance of a new-generation son, Reuben, Leah's firstborn:

Reuben went out during the wheat harvest, found mandrakes in the field, and brought them to his mother Leah. Rachel said to Leah, "Give me some of your son's mandrakes." She answered, "It is bad enough that you have taken my husband, and now you also want to take my son's mandrakes?" Said Rachel, "Then let him sleep with you tonight in exchange of your son's mandrakes." When Jacob came from the field in the evening, Leah went out to him and said, "You are to come to me, for I have paid for you with my son's mandrakes."

This scene is not about the sisters' jealousies, which have been described previously. This scene is about Reuben watching how the flowers he brought his mother – expecting to get a hug – are given to another woman who is frustrating his own mother's desire for her husband. We have here an impressionable child, too young to help with the wheat harvest, learning about the birds and the bees, and shocked by what it means that his mother is married to his father. He sees his sweet mother turn abrasive and give to someone else his gift of the mandrakes. The continual refrain, "my son's mandrakes," makes clear that this is an event in Reuben's life, and we can picture how through similar scenes all the brothers at a tender age are drawn in to the realities of the family structure – now with four wives – each son siding with his own mother's anguish. Such events remain permanently in a boy's consciousness or subconsciousness.

That we are to focus on this scene's psychological aspect is borne out by what follows: "God heard Leah and she became pregnant, giving birth to a fifth son of Jacob. Said Leah, 'God has paid me for giving my maid to my husband.'" If a payback were involved in this birth, it would expectedly be the payback for her giving away her son's mandrakes, with which she bought the right to have Jacob on that night, the night during which she conceived this fifth son. It seems that Leah has blocked this purchase from her conscious mind, perhaps now disturbed by the forwardness she demonstrated in front of Jacob, Rachel, and the tender Reuben. Thus, the focus on the psychological in Reuben's mandrakes scene carries over into the next scene, as Leah subconsciously defends herself against an embarrassing memory.

After working off his fourteen-year bride price, Jacob wants to go home. Laban detains him, so that Jacob works another six years for a share in the profits, again as manager of Laban's flock. Laban constantly tries to cheat Jacob, but God's miracles come to Jacob's aid, and he becomes wealthy. Jacob slips away with his substantial household while Laban is away shearing his sheep. Laban pursues, catches up, and accosts Jacob with an acrid speech, which the reader realizes is an ugly self-portrait:

> What is this you have done, fooling me and stealing away my daughters like captives? Why did you go off stealthily and rob me? You said nothing to me, else I would have given you a festive send-off with singing, drums, and strings. You did not allow me to kiss my sons and daughters ...

The word "steal" appears some ten times in Laban's dealings with Jacob, as an indication of the impossibility of their having an honest relationship. The verbatim exchanges that follow spell out the disengagement of the emerging patriarchal family from its Mesopotamian roots, represented here by Laban. Spelled out in a disengagement agreement are commercial, linguistic, geographic, matrimonial, theological, and ritual aspects.

Laban wants no more theft: "We shall avoid each other ... I shall not advance past this mound toward you ... nor you toward me for wrong." The mound is named by Laban in Aramaic and by Jacob in Hebrew, both meaning "Mound of Witness." The two are shown here separated by language, with Jacob now beyond the Mesopotamian rivers asserting his Hebrew tongue, while Laban maintains his Aramean cultural sphere. Laban had reported to Jacob, "The God of your fathers yesterday said to me, 'Beware not to speak to Jacob either good or evil'" (31:29). But in reporting this warning, how could Laban be upholding God's command? It seems that "not to speak good or evil," is an Aramaic idiomatic expression that conveys noninterference, and Laban himself had used it this way with Abraham's servant in chapter 24.

This discussion took place seven days into Jacob's escape on Mount Gilead, with each party claiming enough mastery over the terrain to name the geographic line of demarcation. In Numbers 32 and Deuteronomy 4, Gilead is a section of Transjordan occupied by the tribes of Menashe and Gad, while in Numbers 36 Gilead is the name of a family of Menashe. Still, it is possible that Gilead is a derivative name that developed from Jacob's Galed, as both are spelled "GLED" in Hebrew.

As part of the agreement, Laban tells Jacob "not to torment my daughters, nor to take wives in addition to my daughters." Of course, Laban himself was the cruel one, keeping Rachel from marrying her fiancé of seven years and then slipping Leah in to a nuptial she had not prepared for. As for more wives, it was Laban's dishonesty that made his daughters into competitors. But the patriarchal family would no longer seek matriarchs of Aramean ancestry, as did Abraham, Isaac, and Jacob. The old racial ties would no longer hold, and a brand new race was in formation. As for Rachel and Leah, early on they demonstrated that they were qualified and ready for a matriarchal role, saying to Jacob: "Do we still have a portion or legacy in our father's home, did he not treat us like strangers, selling us and consuming our bride price? All the wealth that God took from our father belongs to us and our children. And now, do whatever God told you" (31:14).

Still, Rachel did not lose respect or give up on her father. At her departure she stole away her father's images, apparently hoping for him to repent his idolatrous ways. If she had consulted Jacob, he could have told her that nobody changes Laban's mind about anything. At Galed, Laban grills Jacob, "Why did you steal my divinity?" and Rachel hides the fetishes in her camel pack. This matter of religious belief comes up again over the oath Laban proposes for sealing the agreement: "May the God of Abraham and the God of Nahor judge between us – their forefathers' divinities." Jacob is wary of the syncretism in this uneven theological formulation, and Jacob will only swear by He Whom Isaac reveres.

Then Jacob prepares a feast on the mountain and invites "his brethren." The language here has ritual overtones, as if he was preparing a sacrificial meal to which only fellow believers, brethren, would come.

Having extricated himself from Laban, Jacob feels ready to confront Esau, whose anger had been the cause of his stay in Aram. Jacob sends messengers to the Fields of Edom, "He orders them to say, 'Thus shall you say to my master Esau, so says your servant Jacob, I dwelled with Laban, being delayed until now ...'" (32:5). On presenting to Esau, the messengers would include, "Thus shall you say to my master Esau," the standard opening which is evidenced in the salutations of the Sumerian, Mari, and Amarna letters of the time. Jacob calls Esau his master some eight times in the text, but each time it is either to Esau's face or for Esau to hear from the messengers. Otherwise it is plain "Esau" or "my brother Esau." Jacob is trying to make peace by appeasing Esau, by treating him as the royal firstborn, while not trusting him and wishing to have nothing to do with him. Mother Rebecca had feared twenty years earlier that they would kill one another and Jacob is willing to grovel to avoid a bloodbath.

The messengers returned to inform Jacob that Esau was coming to meet him in the company of four hundred men, and Jacob feared an attack. At first blush, we may be puzzled by Jacob's dire reaction. But it may be that the number four hundred here conveys a warning of danger. For it seems that when the number four is specified, as in 4, 14, 40, or 400, it bodes for severity throughout the Book of Genesis. Thus, Abraham's children would be in exile for four hundred years, Ephron cheated Abraham of four hundred shekels, Noah's flood rained down for forty days, Jacob was embalmed lasting forty days, the four Mesopotamian kings came in the fourteenth year and captured Lot. So the reader need only hear four hundred men, while the full report of the messengers would have prompted Jacob's fears.

A thematic word, "*panim*," meaning "face," informs our understanding of Jacob's reunion with his brother. "*Panim*" appears some fifteen times here – four times in a single sentence, verse 21 – with a variety of nuances and idiomatic expressions. Jacob is acting on the face of it, for show, putting a good face on things, saving face, perhaps facetiously. However, the event becomes a serious face-off when Jacob must wrestle at night with a mystery man, who turns out to represent a Divine spirit of confrontation. Jacob overcomes the night-long challenge, and is rewarded by having the spirit bless him with the added name Israel, for his spiritual and physical victory. At sunup, Jacob names the location Peniel, the later Penuel, because "I have come face to face with Divinity and survived."

The thematic word "face" also flanks this event, before and after. When Jacob sets out for the Promised Land, "he rose up, forded the River, and set his face toward Mount Gilead" (31:21). Then after his meeting Esau, "Jacob arrived unharmed at the city of Shechem in the land of Canaan, arriving from Padan Aram, and he camped facing the city" (33:18).

Leaving Penuel, Jacob is limping from where the angel punched his thigh. Suddenly the story jumps to a future time frame, with "This is why the Children of Israel do not eat the sciatic nerve of the hip joint, to this day …" The switch was triggered by the introduction of the name Israel, its first mention. Later, at the time of the Torah's completion, Israel was the name of the national entity – already acknowledged by Pharaoh at the start of Exodus. And Jacob, upon leaving Esau, makes immediate use of the new name in worship, "the Almighty God of Israel" (33:20). Then the name Israel would shortly be confirmed to Jacob in a formal revelation, in chapter 35. But unlike the previous commandment about circumcision, this prohibition against eating the sciatic nerve is not repeated in the prescriptive parts of the Torah. It seems that the reasoning behind this prohibition places it in Genesis, in the wake of creation. For it was only after the flood that humans were elevated over the animals to the extent humans could use animals for food. Now, Jacob the human being *par excellence*, passed muster before the Divine spirit, but his test score was not perfect, as expressed by the injury to his sciatic nerve. Thus, the prohibition against eating this part of the animal symbolizes man's lack of perfection, so that he may not lord it over the animal kingdom totally. So the Book of Genesis is the opus for such an understanding of the Children of Israel's practice to this day.

"This day" may mean the day when there is a People of Israel, in the time of Moses. It may also be taken prophetically as the reader's today, and an identical phrase at the Torah's close, "no one learned his burial place to this day," invites such a reading.

Finally, Esau and Jacob meet and for the moment they are reconciled in earnest, as each "raises his eyes and sees." Still, Jacob also sees Esau's four hundred men and is duly impressed, while Esau sees Jacob's beautiful, orderly family and is duly impressed. In orderly fashion, all the family members bow to Esau, with Rachel bowing last, for she is the family's proud princess and is revolted by this foolery, however necessary her husband claimed it is.

The compliment here to the enviable beauty of Jacob's family makes way for an account of the internal problems that threaten family unity, an explosive issue that will occupy the remainder of the Book of Genesis. This issue comes up at once, in the abduction of Dinah at Shechem.

Shechem, son of Hamor the ruler of the city of Shechem, seized Dinah the daughter of Leah, became infatuated with her, and had his father approach Jacob asking for her hand in marriage. Jacob was dismayed but did nothing until his sons came home, in fury. They answered Hamor deceitfully, claiming they would let Shechem marry their sister if he and all the men of the city would undergo circumcision, so that they could all become one people. The irony here, that the rapist himself would be cutting the very organ with which he violated their sister, was lost on Hamor and his citizens. They all circumcised. Then Dinah's maternal brothers, Simon and Levi, led a surprise attack on the ailing city killing all the men, enslaving the women, taking the booty, and rescuing Dinah. Jacob rebuked Simon and Levi, saying that the nearby Canaanite cities would retaliate mercilessly. They said to Jacob, "Will you let them treat our sister like a prostitute?"

This incident provides a look at the growing breach in the family unity. Dinah was introduced as the child of Leah, and her brothers Simon and Levi also as children of Leah, the wife who repeatedly expressed her pain over being less loved and of a lower status in the family structure. This had just been demonstrated in how Jacob prepared the family for the confrontation with the possibly murderous Esau, "He placed the handmaidens and their children first, Leah and her children last, and Rachel and Joseph last" (33:2). The illogical doubling of "last" indicates the ambivalence in Jacob's balancing his love and his responsibility.

Leah's sons Simon and Levi felt that they and their mother were being discriminated against. They thought that their father's measured response to the outrage against their sister was another indication of how little he thought of their mother's children. Their angry protest was against both Shechem's violation and their father's seeming unconcern. Of course, Jacob had just weathered another agonizing challenge, where he responded with careful appeasement, and he was approaching this new danger with caution. But Simon and Levi could not understand this in their search for self-respect.

An associated disturbance would soon surface, Reuben's affair with Bilhah, Rachel's handmaiden. To minimize Reuben's sin, Bilhah is termed here the father's concubine. Previously, Bilhah and Zilpah were called maidservants, handmaidens, or wives, but not concubines. Reuben's conduct in this affair recalls his childhood involvement in his mother's purchase of a night with his father, using his mandrakes, and the subliminal impact viewing such a scene would make on a tender mind.

When Jacob hears about the Bilhah affair, he does not rebuke Reuben at once, but remembers on his deathbed and renounces Reuben's firstborn status, "because you ventured onto your father's couches." This language includes both a euphemism and an allusion to Reuben's unlucky childhood exposure.

After the debacle at Shechem, God tells Jacob that the time has come for him to return to Bethel, to redeem the pledge he made at "the place," twenty years earlier. God has kept His part of the agreement and has brought Jacob home safely. Jacob arrives at Bethel to worship, when "God ascended off Jacob at the place where He had spoken to him." Such a mystical action was noted with Abraham before his circumcision, as an indication that his freedom of will to circumcise was fully operative, without the powerful influence of a Divine presence. Here too, God had been at Jacob's side through repeated tribulations, but Jacob is left to worship freely, without an overwhelming Divine influence. Then a new revelation renews for Jacob the promises made to Abraham and Isaac for a people and the land, this renewed affirmation made without a reciprocal obligation for worship on Jacob's part.

Left to the forces of nature, Jacob has his beloved Rachel die giving birth to Benjamin, near Bethlehem. He erected a tombstone over her grave, "which is the monument of Rachel's grave to this day." Used for the second time, the phrase "to this day" invites the reader to feel the relevance of the patriarchs and matriarchs for his own world.

Father Isaac's death at age one hundred eighty is noted briefly, with Esau present and prominent at the funeral. At the mention of Esau, the text gives him and his Edomite nation a royal send-off outside the emerging People of Israel.

The text has 43 verses in homage to Esau, with honorable mention of his wives, their respective children, grandchildren – including Amalek – those born in the land of Canaan, those born in the land of Seir, the Hivites of Seir with whom Esau intermarried, personalities who became territorial chieftains, and those who governed Edomite lands in the time of Moses, at the Torah's close.

Also listed, "These are the kings that ruled in the land of Edom before any king ruled for the Children of Israel." Esau's preeminence is flaunted, but by the end of the 43-verse tribute, Esau has been drummed out of "the Children of Israel." The inglorious comparison to the kingship of Edom is the first mention of the kingdom of Israel, and informs the Israelite reader of his own identity. Similarly, Ishmael's exit from a future Israel was respectfully announced in chapter 25, but with less fanfare than is accorded Esau.

While "these are the offspring of Esau," is followed by scores of repeated names, the parallel "These are the offspring of Jacob," offers only one proper name, Joseph. Jacob loves Joseph as he had loved his late mother Rachel, and the brothers, particularly the Leahites, are envious and resentful, with a half-dozen words of hate given in quick succession.

Joseph tells them of dreaming that they were binding grain sheaves in the field and that his brothers' sheaves bowed to his sheaf. The realization of this dream came about when the brothers went down to Egypt for grain. The next dream has the sun, mood, and eleven stars bowing to him, and again this dream was realized when the eleventh brother, Benjamin, was permitted to join the ten for a trip to Egypt.

Meanwhile, Jacob sends Joseph to Shechem, "to check on the peace of your brothers and the peace of the flock." The reader already knows that the brothers "could not talk to him in peace," but Joseph is unaware. He goes on to wander over the pasturelands of Shechem, where a stranger asks what he is looking for. "I am seeking my brothers," is Joseph's answer, which portrays him as at peace with his brothers and unaware of the depth of their hatreds. This innocence was the quality attributed to his father before he became enmeshed with Esau.

The brothers, now in Dothan, spot Joseph from a distance. Excitedly, they scheme to kill him, but Reuben warns against a bloody murder, suggesting that they merely dump him in the deep pit in the desert. Reuben's true motive was to save him, to later draw Joseph from the pit, and to return him to his father. That is, Reuben is acting the part of the responsible firstborn, the nominal leader, who from his childhood has seen how negotiations can hold the troubled family together. But he does not, cannot, stand up against their anger wishing to be rid of Joseph who was threatening their rightful place in the family.

When Joseph reaches them, he finds them ready and waiting, and they quickly drop him into a deep pit. Joseph was astounded, shocked at how they hated him, how they thought his dreams were his aspirations for dominance, how his beloved father had sent him to his death in bowing to his brothers' demands, how hesitant and touching had been the father's two-tiered command, sending him into the clutches of his siblings, perhaps to bring peace to the family. Indeed, prior to sending him off, the last quoted speech has the father shouting at Joseph, "Do you expect me, your mother and brothers to bow down on the ground to you?"

Awaiting death in the pit, a bewildered Joseph concludes that he has been thrown out of the family and that his once-beloved father needed to abandon him. This is the reason why Joseph, later free and powerful in Egypt, does not contact his father, the father who does not want him anymore.

Meanwhile above ground, the brothers sat down to eat, saddened by the thought that one of their own was being put to death, when "they raised their eyes and saw a caravan of Ishmaelites ..." They welcomed Judah's milder proposal of selling Joseph to the approaching Ishmaelites, "instead of our killing him, for he is our brother, our own flesh and blood." But passing Midianite merchants pulled Joseph up and sold him to the Ishmaelites before Judah and his brothers could act. Even earlier, Reuben had slipped away surreptitiously to haul up Joseph, but even Reuven reached the pit belatedly and found the pit empty. The brothers did not know what happened, and agonizingly imagined that a wild animal had attacked him and carried him off. Joseph landed in Egypt as a slave, imagining that his brothers had let the Midianites buy him and sell him to the caravan. On being informed of his beloved son's disappearance, Jacob was inconsolable, crying, "I shall go to my grave as a mourner for my son."

Switching away from this turmoil, the narrative moves to the life of Judah, whose first speech was just recorded at the dispatching of Joseph. Judah's life, like Joseph's to come, will be portrayed here in an existence independent of his brothers and father. As we will soon see, the purpose will be to compare the characters of Judah and Joseph, and that of Reuben as well. We are entering here into the arena of the new generation, and the question of who can take Jacob's place to lead the family.

Judah is introduced as apart from the patriarchal family, his friend is Hirah from Adullam, where he sees a nameless woman – daughter of Shuah – marries her, and he, not she, names their son. But the next two sons are named by the wife, as the spousal relationship seems to improve, and the wife is now given a proper name, Bath-Shuah. When she dies, Judah is in mourning. The Lord is watching, and when Judah's two elder sons sin, the Lord slays them. Moving beyond the tragic deaths, Judah acts confidently to save the third son. Judah suspects Tamar, his twice-widowed daughter-in-law, and he does not let her go through with the traditional levirate marriage to the third son. Indignant, Tamar tricks Judah into fathering a child for her. When the pregnant Tamar is led away to die for her infidelity, she informs Judah that he is the child's father. Judah saves her by admitting, "She is more in the right than I, since I would not give her to my son Shelah." Thus, this free-spirited Judah has the strength of character to accept blame and shame, instead of letting a good woman die.

Tamar goes on to have twins, who grapple in the womb trying to be the firstborn. But these boys will grow up to be loving brothers – unlike Esau and Jacob – so that by the narrative's end Judah is characterized as equal to, and having better children than, the early patriarchs.

Reuben and Joseph too are compared by way of similar involvements, Reuben, as mentioned earlier, in the affair with his father's concubine. Joseph, now successful in Egypt, is tempted by his master's wife. He leaves his jacket in her grasping hands and "he escaped and went outside." (Judah too had handed the harlot, alias Tamar, his scarf as her security.) But his master's wife perceived only that he left his jacket "and ran outside." When she tries to explain to the household servants, she claims that she shouted a

loud protest, "and that he escaped and went outside." Later, showing the jacket to her husband, she reverts to "he *ran* outside." An
escape appears only in those repetitions, which show Joseph in
danger: in the first repetition endangered by the temptation, and
in the third repetition endangered by her supposed shouts. The
incident is presented with such precision to indicate how deep into
trouble Joseph would go in order "not to sin to God."

God is constantly on Joseph's lips, and there is hardly a conversation during which he neglects to mention God, whereas Judah is
not shown as mentioning God during the entire episode devoted
to his life, and only in a response to Joseph will he do so one time
(44:16).

Just as the Lord was there to punish Judah's sons, the Lord was
there to reward Joseph with every success. Even when thrown into
prison by his outraged master, Joseph soon interprets a dream for
the imprisoned butler, who later reports to Pharaoh that "a Hebrew lad" in prison can explain Pharaoh's puzzling dreams.

On hearing Pharaoh's dreams about the fat and lean cows and
grains, Joseph's first words were, "Pharaoh dreamed a single
dream." The Egyptian soothsayers could not say this, and that is
why they were unable to interpret the dream satisfactorily.

For the Egyptian believer, the cow was a sacred object and was
not to be eaten, "the Egyptians could not eat with the Hebrews"
(43:32), and the "Egyptians abominated all those who pasture
flocks" (46:34). The grain of Pharaoh's dream obviously represented food for man and beast, so that the soothsayers could not
conceive of a parallel between the sacred cows and the profane
grains, and see it as a single repeated message. But how could
Joseph transgress the Egyptian belief system? He overcame this
problem by declaring "God is informing Pharaoh of His plans."
That is, if the Egyptians expect a divine representation, it appears
for them in the half of the dream with the cows. Of course, for
Joseph the Hebrew, the parallel between the cow and grain is food.
To satisfy the Egyptian theology, Joseph repeats five times that
the dream is a message from God. But Joseph is careful not to say
anything negative about their sacred cows, even the ugly cows, and
only in connection with the seven wilted grains does he predict the
seven years of famine (41:27).

Divinity remains central to the interpretation as Joseph goes on to tell Pharaoh that it is God advising him to save the grain of the fat years for the coming lean years, and that Pharaoh should appoint someone to oversee this effort. That Pharaoh accepts Joseph's twist on the Egyptian mindset is indicated by Pharaoh's responding with mention of God, "Is there anyone like this who has in him the spirit of God? . . . Since God has told you all this . . . you shall oversee my house and your orders shall provide for my people."

Thus, it is due to Pharaoh's need to justify the divine aspect of the dream that Joseph is elevated to a governor. The unbelievability of anyone going from prisoner to viceroy is mitigated by having Pharaoh's appointment of Joseph repeated almost a dozen times by either a direct order, such as "See, I have put you over all the land of Egypt," or by a demonstrative act, such as "Pharaoh removed the ring from his hand and placed it in Joseph's hand." Finally, given a wife too, Joseph began the job.

When the seven years of famine begin in Canaan, Jacob sends his sons, minus Benjamin, to buy grain in Egypt. There, Joseph himself apparently checked on foreign delegations for possible spies. He sees his ten brothers and confronts them haltingly. He is not sure why they don't recognize him, for don't they recall how they sent him off to Egypt as a slave? Seeing them bow to him, Joseph is flooded with the memory of his youthful dreams – dreams that he had flushed from his mind together with the painful memories of his father. And when Joseph had rejoiced over the birth of his first son in Egypt, he had thanked God for helping him forget his once-happy existence in his father's home.

"You are spies," said Joseph with dramatic irony, meaning you are a bunch of criminals who would kill or kidnap a brother.

"No, we are all sons of one father, honest men who were never spies," they answer, thinking that Joseph's accusation is based on their large number.

"No, you come to spy out the land," responds Joseph, contradicting their having said that all of them there, including Joseph, are sons of one father – the father that disowned him – and also contradicting the switch to the past tense, for assuredly they were criminals when they sold him.

"But your servants are twelve brothers, sons of one father in Canaan, the youngest one there with our father, and one is no more," they say, imagining that their large number is still the problem.

"Indeed, it is as I told you, you are spies," said Joseph, contradicting their assertion that he himself, the twelfth brother, is no more, for he is right there. Joseph orders them to bring Benjamin as proof that they are not spies. This test makes no sense to the brothers, but for Joseph it would mean that they are no longer capable of dispatching another son of Rachel en route.

Perplexed, the brothers blurt out that they are now being punished for what they had done to Joseph. Reuben adds, "Did I not tell you not to harm the boy, but you wouldn't listen." Reuben's self-righteousness is not borne out by the original account, where Reuben had lied to them about his intention to save Joseph. Still, when Joseph overhears this Hebrew conversation he takes not Reuben but Simon, the next oldest, as the hostage. For Joseph, overhearing this conversation began a step-by-step discovery of what really had happened to land him in Egypt.

On hearing their expressions of sorrow, Joseph hid away and cried, as cry he would each successive time his anger mellowed. He now let them take the grain needed for their starving families back home, gave them food for the road, and had their payments returned secretly to their grain packs, in a silent act of rapprochement.

Back home, the brothers report the viceroy's demands to the father, knowing full well that Jacob would refuse to trust them with his beloved Benjamin. But with his refusal, Jacob declares himself of equal concern for all his sons, "You have bereaved me, Joseph is gone, Simon is gone, and now you would take Benjamin." The brothers quote Joseph as having said to them, "Bring me your young brother so that I will know that you are not spies ... then you may establish commerce in the land." The enticement of commercial rights was a ploy that Hamor of Shechem had tried to use against them, and the brothers' attempt to use it against Jacob mirrors their exasperation.

Then Reuben tells Jacob, "You may kill my two sons if I do not bring him back to you." The father is unmoved and the brothers do not support Reuben's attempt because they see it as another of Reuben's self-righteous declarations, as if to say that only he is innocent of the violence done to Joseph: For the second son offered by Reuben corresponds to Joseph, whose loss Reuben blames them for.

Eventually, Judah tries to persuade the father, using a business-like tone and speaking as if an equal. The brothers do support Judah, so that the father is finally ready to risk it, adding a prayer, and a gift of Holy Land delicacies for the viceroy.

Reaching Egypt, they become apprehensive on learning that they were invited to dinner with the viceroy. At dinner they wonder if the viceroy too is a Hebrew of sorts, for the Egyptians will not eat his fare either. They find themselves seated according to their seniority, and they marvel. This display of the right of seniority – repeated by Joseph on three occasions – is Joseph engaging in a secret denial of the accusation that his youthful dreams were destroying the family order, based on respect for age. On the other hand, Joseph handed the younger Benjamin five times more presents during the meal than the other brothers, perhaps to justify his right, or his father's right, to have an emotional preference and to love. And when Joseph first noticed Benjamin there with them, he had to go to his private chamber for an emotional cry.

Next morning, Joseph sends them home, but has a servant slip a silver goblet into Benjamin's grain sack. Joseph then sends the servant to catch them beyond the city limits and accuse them of stealing Joseph's diviner chalice, asking "Why have you repaid good with evil?" Joseph re-enacts for them a scene of pursuit that they had experienced together in childhood when Laban had pursued them, accused them of stealing his idols, subjected them to a methodic search, and terrorized them with the fear of his finding the idols, which Rachel had hidden under her camel seat. As in the case of Laban's idols, the brothers' retort was that whoever stole the chalice could be killed and that they all would be Joseph's slaves.

The magic chalice is found in Benjamin's sack, and Joseph needles them, "Shouldn't you have known that a man like me would be a diviner?" At this point Joseph is not only lying, but misrepresenting his own essence as a true God-fearing man. Judah's response, "We cannot justify ourselves, for God has uncovered our prior sin," constitutes a reversal of roles: Judah was never before quoted as mentioning God, while Joseph, who mentions God over a dozen times, is here passing himself off as a mere soothsayer. This Judah is bound to win over this Joseph.

Joseph tells them that only the thief will remain as an Egyptian slave, while the rest of them may leave for Canaan. From the start Joseph's hidden plan was to isolate Benjamin, reveal himself as his real brother, tell him how heartless the rest of the family is, and invite Benjamin to join his true brother in a life of righteousness and luxury in Egypt.

Judah's purpose was just the opposite. He was prepared to remain as a substitute slave in Egypt as long as Benjamin returned home to his loving father. That Judah had the strength of character to accept blame and pain, rather than let his father perish, was already demonstrated in the Tamar episode when he accepted blame and shame rather than let Tamar die unjustly.

Judah confronts Joseph with a plea that goes back to the beginning, using his own interpretation of events. That Joseph had accused them of spying, that Joseph now accuses them of stealing, he omits as baseless. Judah's retelling is supported by the precise words used when the brothers reported back to Jacob, such as "Do not come see me unless your young brother is with you," "The lad cannot leave his father or he will die," "If I don't bring him back to you I will be a sinner to father all my life."

But Judah repeats a quote of Jacob's that astounds Joseph: "You know that my wife bore me two sons. One is gone and methinks that he was savaged, for I have not seen him until now, and now you want to take this other one and something will happen to him too ..." Joseph has just learned that his father did not conspire with the Leahites to dispose of him, that his father did not reject him, that instead his father was in mourning over his loss, and that he loved him and Benjamin.

Joseph's short ejaculation, "I am Joseph – is my father still alive!" is pregnant with interior meaning. For one, he marvels that he too has a father and that he was not rejected into fatherlessness as he had imagined all these years. Secondly, Joseph was horrified to realize that he had been tormenting his father – as Judah was unwilling to do – by jumping to the conclusion that his father had wanted him out of the family, which is why Joseph had not contacted him from Egypt. Thirdly, that since his elderly father was still alive, Joseph could rejoice with him once more.

After regaining composure, Joseph addresses his shrinking brothers with his version of events: "I am your brother Joseph whom you sold into Egypt. Don't be sorry because it was God who sent me to sustain you, as this famine continues beyond these two years ... God has made me a counselor to Pharaoh ... Go tell my father of my importance in Egypt ... and quickly bring my father down here."

After initial disbelief, Jacob is willing to move to Egypt so as to ride out the famine. "Magnificent that my son Joseph is still alive. I shall go to see him before I die." Here again as on each occasion that Jacob mentions Joseph, it has life-and-death significance. But leaving the Holy Land is no small matter, so Jacob first visits Beer-Sheva to render sacrifice to God. In a vision God tells Jacob, "Do not be afraid of going down to Egypt, for I shall make you into a great nation there...."

What follows is a count of seventy Israelite persons who accompany Jacob to Egypt. The organization of the census is complex and it signifies the central issue of the remainder of the Book of Genesis; namely, how Jacob's family will stay together there and how they will organize themselves so they remain distinct.

The count begins by naming 33 offspring of Leah, with Jacob himself the 33. Then the 16 offspring of Zilpah. Continuing in descending order, the 14 of Rachel, "the wife of Jacob." Then Bilhah's 7 sons and grandsons. The initial impression is that each individual is equal, that the greater the number the greater its importance. Thus, Leah's 33 come first and father Jacob is counted with Leah's group.

Unexpectedly, a new total of 66 is given for those actually accompanying Jacob on his trip and those "born of Jacob's loins." This count eliminates Joseph and his two sons who were already in Egypt, and eliminates Jacob who was not "born of Jacob's loins." To reach the total of seventy souls, one must now add Joseph with his two sons and Jacob himself! The question is quietly being raised as to whom Jacob belongs: to Leah's majority or to Rachel's beloved sons?

When the census concludes we read, "And he sent Judah before him to Joseph to arrange for him in Goshen." This "he" obviously refers to Jacob, but his name as the grammatical referent last appeared before the census, in "Jacob arose from BeerSheva," or in "These are the names of the Children of Israel coming to Egypt, Jacob and his sons." Thus, the census is presented parenthetically, surrounded by Jacob's presence and asking where he belongs and who can best represent him to lead the family. The answer here is Judah. Judah, unlike the firstborn Reuben, was able to get the brothers to listen to him, Judah was able to win the father's trust about Benjamin, Judah was able to deal with the delicate Tamar issue, and Judah was able to stand up to the viceroy of Egypt, Joseph.

Along these lines, the objective tone of the census provides an instructive detail regarding Dinah: "These are the sons of Leah that she bore to Jacob in Padan Aram, and Dinah *his* daughter." The wording is comparable to the start of chapter 35, "Dinah the daughter of *Leah* that she bore to Jacob, went out … ," where Dinah is called Leah's daughter, because this was why her brothers Simon and Levi accused Jacob of being insensitive to her and them. But the census corrects this partisan view of calling Dinah his daughter.

On Jacob's arrival, Joseph rides out to meet them and characteristically sobs, while Jacob repeats his poignant mantra, "Now I can die, having seen your face, that you are alive." As required, Joseph introduces the brothers to Pharaoh, but conspired to have them identify themselves as mere shepherds seeking pasture in Goshen during the hunger. In the same spirit, when the aged Jacob is presented to Pharaoh, Jacob explains, "My wandering days amount to a hundred thirty years, few and troublesome when compared to the lengthy years of my forefathers' days of settlement." Naturally Pharaoh and his court did not relish the company of downbeat foreigners, and Joseph succeeded in keeping his family from being sucked into the Egyptian ruling class and culture.

Joseph took care of the whole family's basic needs but he also minded his job conscientiously and competently, directing the country's response to the famine. The populace was grateful to him for his considerate management, which the text reports in fifteen long verses, and Joseph's rulings "became law until this very day."

The patriarch Jacob saw it as a problem. For should his favorite son – who was committed to both Israel's and Egypt's wellbeing – become the next patriarch, the Israelites might merge with the Egyptians, as happened to Esau's family when it settled in Seir with the Horites. The remainder of Jacob's life will be devoted to an energetic response to this problem, toward assuring the family's integrity after he is gone.

"Jacob lived one hundred forty-seven years," the text states but surprisingly goes on to tell of Jacob's living activity for another 57 verses, involving four major initiatives. It soon becomes clear that this Jacob is engaged in preparing the family's continuity after his death. Here Jacob is putting aside his personal life, his interests, his passion, his preference, in order to mold the family into a harmonious entity. Judah must be named leader, but he is wary lest Joseph, who is presently in charge of the family, takes umbrage and feels so distanced that he breaks away.

Jacob calls in Joseph and asks him not to have him buried in Egypt but to inter him in their forefathers' sepulcher. Of course, such a burial in the Holy Land would make a statement about Israel's continued attachment there, even after Israel's emigration, and about the continuity of the patriarchal tradition in death as in life. Joseph answers, "I myself shall do as you say." Jacob is wary of the added "myself" and he makes Joseph swear it. Indeed, when eventually the father dies, we will see how difficult it becomes for Joseph to give up his father, "He fell on his father's face, wept and kissed him. He ordered the doctors to embalm his father … It took forty days. Then for seventy days Egypt mourned him. . . ." Then Joseph approached Pharaoh's court to get permission from Pharaoh to go to Canaan. Permission granted, Joseph declared another seven days of mourning en route in Transjordan. So Jacob understood that an oath was in order to tie Joseph's hands and prevent him from keeping his beloved father with him. Joseph swears and Jacob bows to his son in gratitude, fulfilling the dream that showed the sun and moon bowing to Joseph. As for the dream's moon, Rachel, she will feature in Jacob's next initiative.

At Jacob's next visit, Jacob again brings up the Holy Land, where Joseph had not lived since he was a teen-aged boy. Jacob tells him that Almighty God had given the Holy Land to him and to his children forever: "Now the two sons born to you before I came here to you in Egypt are mine; Ephraim and Menashe are just like Reuben and Simon for me." The logic that Jacob is pressing upon Joseph is that although you were away from the family heritage all these years, and I missed you dearly, I shall consider you as having lived there with us, so that the two sons you bore while away shall be considered native sons. Further, I award you, through these two, the firstborn's double portion in the Promised Land.

Then Jacob turns the subject back to their previous discussion, the matter of burial, of course burial in the Promised Land: "As for me, when I arrived from Padan Aram I lost my Rachel there in Canaan a short distance from Ephrath, and I buried her there on the way to Ephrath." Suddenly Jacob stops, interrupted by seeing others in the room who might overhear his sensitive remarks. He is told that Joseph's two sons are in the room, and he turns to them instead. What more would Jacob have said if he had not been interrupted? He might have said: "Joseph, I don't want you to bury me next to your mother, but in the Duplex Cave at Mamre next to Leah in the patriarchal sepulcher. This is needed for the tradition and for the integrity of the ongoing family. When your dear mother died, we had just survived the dangerous confrontation with Esau, I called him my master and superior, and I could not claim for my Rachel the rights to the family plot while he was still about with his four-hundred men; so I buried your mother at Ephrath." But Jacob felt that this would not sit well with this son, and Jacob would never again broach the subject with Joseph privately. He now turned to a sounder approach to Joseph's sympathies: "Bring me your sons so I can bless them."

"Israel extended his right hand and placed it on the head of Ephraim, who was the younger, then placed his left hand on the head of Menashe, crossing his hands. . . . Joseph said to his father, 'No father, this is the firstborn, place your right hand on him.' His father refused saying, 'I know, my son, and he too shall be a great nation, but his younger brother will be greater, with his descendants filling the earth.' And he blessed them."

Joseph here is trying to avoid having his sons endure the terrible relationship he had with his brothers and is expressing the view that if recognition of the elder is properly followed there will be no jealousy. Joseph expressed this sentiment on three previous occasions as well. But Jacob is instead making a statement for the rights of excellence, talent, and success. Shortly, Jacob will be using his approach to harmony in his next undertaking, when he calls the family together for his last will and testament. And of course, if Joseph's policy had been followed, Jacob himself would not have gotten Isaac's blessing, and Esau would be the patriarch instead. Besides, the firstborn Menashe was named with the hope that Joseph could then forget the latent memories of his father's home, and the significance of names is prominent in the upcoming family conclave.

Going into the assembly, Jacob has already given Joseph the double portion of the birthright and the patriarchal blessings, each of which cost him dearly because he had wrested them from Esau. Will Joseph be satisfied? Will the recognition accompanying these gifts placate the family's provider and viceroy of Egypt, if Jacob appoints a leader who can better hold the family together? There are three contenders, Reuben, Judah, and Joseph. Only these three will be addressed directly, in the second person, while the remaining brothers are spoken about, using the third person. Jacob must choose Judah but he must present the decision as fair.

First mention goes to Reuben the firstborn. Jacob eliminates him by citing the long-forgotten affair with the concubine Bilhah. At the time, Jacob said nothing, Reuben continued to function as the firstborn, and Jacob had mentioned him approvingly just a dozen verses before the conclave. But Jacob is using a pretext to eliminate him, while the real reason is that Reuben would not succeed in leadership based on past performance.

Continuing in order of seniority, Jacob eliminates Simon and Levi because of their surprise attack on Shechem. Their motive had been a partisan one, demanding more respect for their mother Leah and her children. But needed was a leader who would transcend the four-way maternal division of the family and be above partisan suspicion. At the time they had answered Jacob nastily, but here just five verses back, Jacob expressed approval of armed conquest of the Promised Land. Their elimination was needed to bring forward Judah, the next eldest.

There is nothing wrong with Judah, he is the next eldest, and he is being proclaimed the future leader – fair is fair, using Joseph's own guidelines. At Judah's birth Leah had exclaimed, "This time I will merely thank the Lord," in simple gratitude without regard to the competition expressed in the names of the other sons. It would be this son who transcends the envy to lead a unified family.

In selecting Judah, Jacob adds a nuance to his name: Judah, to mean a confirmation of majesty and glory. He proceeds then to bless him with a glorious land, and from this point in Jacob's oration each son will receive a blessing. Next comes Zebulun who had been named in the hope "that now my husband will dwell with me." Jacob renames him as dwelling along the shore with ships at Sidon.

Issachar had been named as the reward for sharing a husband, and Jacob renames him for the rewards of honest labor in a pleasant land, comparing him to a powerful mule. Next Dan, who was named for God's favorable decision in granting this son, is now named a judge who renders honest decisions for Israel and, like a serpent, will defend Israel from lawless invaders.

Here Jacob has passed the halfway mark in addressing the sons. He has been saving Joseph, with Benjamin, for last, and the real test of his peacemaking is fast approaching. Anxiously, he turns to God in prayer, "O Lord I seek Your help." The next three sons, leading to Joseph, are dealt with in single, brief parallel poetic lines, each having two short stanzas indicating that the call for Divine help is needed for the approaching Joseph, who will merit a full 5-verse statement, equal to the full 5-verse selection of Judah.

The first of the three is Gad, who was named for the lucky company of another child. Now he is renamed for a military company, providing defense. Asher was named for the delight of yet another son, and here renamed for his earth's delightful fruit, delectables worthy of a king. Naphtali was named for winning in the contest for sons, and here he is compared to a racing hind, winning applause. There is a musicality to these three short verses: The "l" of Naphtali is sounded three times, the "m" sound is found five times in Asher's seven words, and the "d" of Gad is heard five times in six words.

Finally to Joseph. When Rachel had Joseph she asked God for yet more sons, Joseph's name conveying an increase. Here Jacob pictures him as a prolific lad at a spring-well, with the girls prancing about. It was at a spring-well that the matriarchs met their husbands. Jacob expresses his sympathy for Joseph by recognizing that the brothers had antagonized him, but that Joseph was victorious. The victory, Jacob tells him, came thanks to the God of his father, yes of Jacob, yes of Israel. Then Jacob again pronounces the forefathers' blessings he had already given him in private and adds, "Your father's blessings streak beyond my parents' blessings, reaching the peak of eternal passion." He ends by calling Joseph "the saintly brother," mentioning "brother" in the hope that Joseph will consider himself part of a brotherhood having other prominent members.

The remaining Benjamin is treated in one quick verse of less than ten words, having the same three-phrase structure as Zebulun's, which followed upon the important address to Judah. Jacob's early attachment to Benjamin was predicated upon his being thought the sole survivor of the beloved Rachel. In fact, the text never grants Benjamin a single quoted speech. But here Jacob is brushing aside the love of his life in order to insure the life of the family.

The very next verse testifies that Jacob had succeeded in cementing the family: "All these are the twelve tribes of Israel, and this is what their father said to them, blessing them, each with a fitting blessing." There remained Jacob's fourth and final initiative before his death, this one directed at the sons jointly:

I am about to die, bury me with my forefathers in the cave of Ephron the Hittite's field, the cave of the duplex field near Mamre in Canaan, which Abraham bought from Ephron the Hittite for a cemetery. There did they bury Abraham and Sarah his wife, there did they bury Isaac and Rebecca his wife, and there did I bury Leah.

While he had Joseph swear previously not to bury him in Egypt but in Canaan, here in the company of all the brothers Jacob spells out that the burial is to be next to Leah, even as he omits the expected "my wife."

As viceroy, the bereaved Joseph takes over the elaborate funeral arrangements. In requesting permission from Pharaoh for the trip, Joseph reports Jacob's instructions as, "Bury me in the sepulcher I prepared in Canaan," omitting the named Duplex Cave. Joseph starts out accompanied by Egypt's cavalry, the officials, the elders, a multitude of the citizenry – and his brothers. The international reaction saw the huge funeral procession as an Egyptian event. "This is a grievous loss for Egypt," onlookers said in Transjordan.

What was the procession doing in Transjordan, when the direct route was the southern coastal road "through the land of the Philistines" (Exodus 13:17)? And why the seven-day delay in Transjordan? Were they wandering about and was there a problem? As a son of Rachel, Joseph may have had a problem, and if the funeral procession passed Ephrath from the North before reaching Mamre to the South and Joseph buried his father next to his mother Rachel, no one could have stopped hm. But the influence of the brothers prevailed: "His sons did for him what he had commanded them. His sons carried him to Canaan, they buried him in the cave of the duplex field near Mamre which Abraham had bought from Ephron the Hittite for a burial ground" (50:12).

A sigh of relief is felt in the sentence that follows: "So Joseph returned to Egypt, he and his brothers, and all who went with him to bury his father, after they had buried his father." Whew! But the old wounds that had divided the family along maternal lines had again been pricked, and the brothers feared, "Perhaps Joseph hates us and will repay us for all the evil we did to him." They go beg Joseph for forgiveness, "We are your slaves." Joseph responds by crying with them in brotherly fashion and consoles them with an old phrase of their father's, "What, am I in the place of God?"

At the approach of his own death, Joseph calls the now harmonious brothers together and asks that when God finally returns Israel to the Holy Land, they take his embalmed bones with them – like father. The death of Joseph is dwelt upon in five full verses, the last of the Book of Genesis. This emphasis on Joseph's passing contributes to the book's closure. For the reader of Genesis, the most poignant scene was the introduction of human mortality, that everyone from Adam to the reader himself must die. The book's final scene reasserts this reality, in that even the righteous Joseph – a servant of God – is mortal like the rest of us.

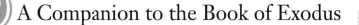

PART II

A Companion to the Book of Exodus

"AND THESE ARE THE names of the Children of Israel who came to Egypt ..." *And?* Is this the way to start a new book, with "and"? The answer is that Exodus begins by quoting a line from Genesis, and this line properly began with "and" where it appeared in Genesis 46:8. This phrase is an appropriate start for Exodus because the book centers on the redemption from Egypt, so the narrative starts with the trip from Canaan to Egypt.

The Torah is not one book that is then divided conveniently into five parts. Rather the Torah comprises a series of five books, each with its central theme, message, rhetoric, beginning, and ending. Accordingly, each of the last four books ends with a summary close, referring to all its commandments or to all Israel. Deuteronomy is introduced as a distinct book, which contains the speeches of Moses to all Israel. Still, each new book acknowledges the content of the prior book – as with the Exodus quote from Genesis – and there is a basic chronological order to the series. (Nachmanides, in the better editions of his *Commentary to the Torah*, explains the beginning of Exodus along these lines.)

But the quote from Genesis soon changes to paraphrase, to the sounding of key words, and to telescoping, so that the Exodus beginning does not mirror the concerns of the earlier version, as indeed even the order of the twelve tribes is changed. The opening paragraph concludes with what has already been noted in Genesis

47:27, that Israel "multiplied and became exceedingly numerous," but the Exodus version uses three times as many words to emphasize that "the land swarmed with them." This incremental repetition prepares us for Exodus' first wholly new fact: that the King of Egypt became alarmed by so many Hebrews, which he termed a nation, its first such recognition.

In terms of broad sweep, Exodus begins where Genesis left off. Genesis had begun with only the presence of God, who then created a world with living beings, particularly human beings to whom God related. Bit by bit, the narrative switches more to the activities of humankind and less to Divine initiatives. Thus, the last Divine revelation in Genesis happens five chapters before the end, and the revelation that preceded that one happened ten chapters before that. Exodus opens into a world wherein God is not mentioned. In charge is the King of Egypt. Indeed, that he is not called Pharaoh initially, as expected, but a king, lends weight to the characterization of this king as a competitor to the Divine and a symbol for an anti-god culture. Just as this king did not know Joseph, he goes on to blaspheme, "I do not know the Lord" (5:2). It is into such a world that Exodus opens and the challenge facing the book is how to bring the Divine into a world of evil – for the ruling King of Egypt is a murderer of children. It is the nation of the Children of Israel who become charged with justifying Divinity's return to center stage.

In terms of its broad sweep, Exodus moves in an opposite direction from Genesis. Exodus begins with a godless world and ends at the other extreme with "The Lord's glory filling the Tabernacle" (20:35). The Children of Israel's devotion made it possible for Divinity to fill the earth once more.

Womankind in Genesis was not given a particularly heroic role, but in Exodus the women are the perpetual heroines. The two midwives are the first to stand up to the King of Egypt, refusing to kill the boys and answering the evil monarch wisely. Then a brave mother manages to hide her newborn for three months and then saves him with floating a box in the Nile, calling him Moses meaning, "I drew him up from the water." Moses' sister knew exactly what to say to the Egyptian princess, and the princess and her maids too were merciful women. Later in Exodus women repeatedly get favorable mention, as when Miriam led the women in the Song of the Sea, when Tzipora saved Moses' life by circumcising their son, and when the women's contributions to the Tabernacle are mentioned over a half-dozen times, in chapter thirty-five. So starting with the midwives, the women of Exodus are credited with the rectification of mankind's world and ushering in the Divine glory.

Moses is the hero central to the Book of Exodus from beginning to end. Introduced as the son of a nameless Levite couple, Moses is brought up by both his birth mother and the Egyptian princess who found him. He matures into a man who will not stand by and countenance a wrong being done. When he sees an Egyptian beating a Hebrew – now one of his "brethren" – Moses kills the Egyptian. The next day, on seeing two Hebrew men wrangling, Moses intervenes to help the victim, and is told by the Hebrew fellow to mind his own business. Later wanted for killing the Egyptian, Moses escapes to Midian. At the well, he sees the local shepherds driving off a group of seven girl shepherdesses and Moses comes to their aid. Even as a runaway in a strange land Moses came forward to right a wrong. It was this man that God would choose as the human partner in His undertaking to bring Israel out of Egypt.

God's decision to act on His promises for redemption concludes with, "God heard their groans and recalled His covenant with Abraham, Isaac, and Jacob. God saw the Children of Israel and God knew" (2:24). This series of hearing, seeing, and knowing is repeated a half-dozen times, with variations, between this first-time use and the end of chapter four, "The people believed [acknowledged] when they heard that the Lord remembered the Children of Israel and that He saw their pain, and they made obeisance."

This series provides a theological metaphor for noting three steps in the Divine decision-making. The *hearing* portrays a distant human-like initial awareness, the *seeing* points to a view that transcends from the imagined heaven down to earth, and the *knowing* is the absolute, with God knowing what to do. Additionally, *seeing* is a thematic word on its own. It appears a half-dozen times from the birth of Moses to his slaying the Egyptian, then another ten times when Moses sees the burning bush and God appears to him.

There is in Genesis another thematic phrase that involves see-ing, "Raise up your eyes and see." This phrase occurs a dozen times in Genesis but not a single time in Exodus, where *seeing* is projected via the hearing, seeing, knowing series.

The angel of the Lord calls to Moses from the burning bush and tells him to join with God in freeing Israel from Egypt. Moses does not want to, he feels unworthy. What follows is a test of wills between man and God, each proceeding with his essential nature. God wishes to convince Moses, but He will not interfere with man's essential free will. God begins to describe the need to rescue Israel from oppression, as Moses has always been responsive to such an appeal, and God offers proof for the success of the mission, "that when you take the people out of Egypt, you shall worship God on this mountain." For the Divine, the future and present are the same, and the mountain was already termed the Mountain of God because of the future Sinai revelation, and God assures Moses, "I shall be with you." But for Moses, the human, God's appeal to future events is unconvincing. When Moses asks for the name and aspect of Divinity he is to convey to the Israelites, God retorts, "I shall be what I shall be," as a rejoinder to Moses for being un-impressed with the Almighty's knowledge of the future. But soon God relents and reveals the Tetragrammaton, the Lord's personal name and essential aspect.

Still Moses says no and asks God to send someone else. It turns out that one of the reasons for Moses' refusal was consideration for his older brother Aaron, who was in Egypt and already a leading Levite elder, and Moses did not want to upstage him nor arouse any jealousy. In response, God tells Moses, "I know that your brother Aaron the Levite will willingly speak, and he is coming to meet you and his heart will rejoice at seeing you ... He will be your mouthpiece and you will be his god." While unenthusiastic, Moses finally agrees.

That Moses had the audacity to refuse God, reminds us of the parallel scene where Abraham confronts God over the impending destruction of Sodom, in Genesis 18. Just as there Abraham was facing but a proxy for God in the form of Abraham's third visitor, here too Moses is arguing with God's proxy calling from the burn-ing bush. Accordingly, both Abraham and Moses address God as

"Master" (spelled *Adonoy*) during the disputation, an indication of a respectful distance from essential Divinity.

Still hesitant in Midian, Moses asks his father-in-law for permission "to go see if my brethren in Egypt are still alive." Surprisingly, permission is granted. God urges Moses twice more in Midian, once assuring him that those who were hunting for him in Egypt have died, and a second time with a speech for Pharaoh warning him that Israel is the Lord's firstborn son and that if Pharaoh detains Israel, the Lord will slay Pharaoh's firstborn son. So Moses starts out for Egypt, but again tarries at a wayside inn, and God threatens to slay him – for death had been mentioned and was now on the agenda. Tzipora, Moses' wife, saves the day by quickly circumcising their newborn son, thereby providing an excuse for their slow progress.

Then Aaron arrives, kisses Moses, and is delighted that God has chosen his younger brother. This brotherly love bodes well for their venture, and it declares that the envy that had plagued successive brothers in Genesis has been overcome. With great enthusiasm they say to Pharaoh, "So says the Lord God of Israel: Let my people go...." Pharaoh refuses. Apparently, in their sudden enthusiasm they had neglected to use the language God had prescribed in chapter 3, verse 18. Correcting themselves they say, "The God of the Hebrews called to us...." But the mission had failed and Pharaoh ordered the taskmasters to work the Hebrews harder. The overworked Israelites, now restless, upbraid Moses for making things worse. In turn, Moses complains to God, "Master, why are You hurting these people and why did You send me? Since my coming to Pharaoh in Your name, things are worse for these people, neither did You redeem Your people."

God responds with a lengthy rebuke, patiently explaining the history and meaning of the Divine promise made to the patriarchs for the return of their children to their own Holy Land. There is then a break in the ongoing narrative in order to reintroduce Moses, who finally is committed to God's enterprise. Initially, Moses had been introduced without fanfare, an unknown. Here he and Aaron – perhaps because of Aaron – are placed in the glorious context of the Chosen People, having pedigree ancestors and marrying prominent women. Aaron's genealogy covers six generations, some into future time, so that the genealogical intrusion may be signaling the Eternal's appreciation of Moses and Aaron, despite Moses' bold initial resistance to God's call.

God was about to unleash the ten plagues against Egypt, and He charged Moses as follows: "See here, I am appointing you Pharaoh's lord, with Aaron your brother as your prophet. You shall convey whatever I tell you and Aaron your brother shall tell Pharaoh to release the Children of Israel from his land. And I will harden the heart of Pharaoh so as to multiply my signs and wonders in Egypt. Pharaoh will not listen to you, then I will clamp My hand down on Egypt and redeem My hosts, My people, the Children of Israel from Egypt with mighty justice. Egypt will learn that I am the Lord when I flex My arm over Egypt and remove the Children of Israel from its midst" (9:1).

What follows is a contest between Pharaoh and Moses, and it is the contest form that allows Pharaoh to persevere through the ten plagues. If God's hardening of Pharaoh's heart is taken just literally then the drama of the ten plagues becomes a meaningless charade. That Divine justice does not tamper with man's freedom of will was already demonstrated when Moses refused God's order initially. But by having Moses and Aaron negotiate with Pharaoh, he is allowed to stubbornly maintain his imagined control, his authority as king and demigod under Egyptian culture. Thus, the first miracles are such that the magicians can duplicate, and Pharaoh goes on to view Moses and Aaron as merely better magicians. Exuding cooperation, Moses asks Pharaoh when he wants the frogs to depart, Pharaoh bravely says tomorrow, and so it was. Pharaoh is given the impression that Moses can control or is able to time natural disasters, by extending his staff to start a plague and by praying publicly to have God withdraw a plague. Indeed, God uses nature to harness the plagues, leaving Pharaoh to wonder if his troubles are not due to natural causes. The locusts were brought in by the east wind and removed by a west wind. The plagues were so varied that they did not give the impression of a unified Divine attack. A likely contemporary Egyptian papyrus bemoans the woes that befell Egypt as being a series of national calamities.

Moses claimed that he was only asking permission to go to the desert for three days in order to worship the God of the Hebrews, a minimal request that would not overwhelm Pharaoh. Moses sounded like a reasonable negotiator when he explained, "Can we slaughter the deities of the Egyptians before their very eyes without them stoning us? Let us go a three-day journey into the desert to sacrifice to the Lord our God …" (8:22). Similarly, Pharaoh seemed a reasonable negotiator when he argued that wanting to take along the little children and flock was out of the question, for we read in Genesis 50, on the trip to bury Jacob, "Only the little children, the flocks, and the cattle did they leave behind in Goshen." Moses seemed pliable enough, since whenever he was asked to stop an ongoing plague he cooperated.

God's hardening of the heart of Pharaoh was the indirect result of the process, of the contest between Moses and Pharaoh. Pharaoh was able to be stubborn because God withheld His omnipotent glory – until the final plague of slaying the firstborn. All along, the suffering Egyptian citizen saw Moses – and his fellow Hebrews – as a friend who put a stop to each successive annoyance when asked: "The Lord made the Egyptians look kindly on the people, and the man Moses, too, was very prominent in Egypt, in the eyes of Pharaoh's servants and the citizenry" (11:3). Was not Moses good enough to warn them to stay inside before the hailstorm? It was only when Pharaoh finally realized that Moses was intractable that he ordered him to stay away, on pain of death.

The same indirect process for hardening Pharaoh's heart is operative at the crossing of the Red Sea in chapter 14: "Speak to the Children of Israel and let them go back and camp at Pi HaHiroth … so that Pharaoh can say that the Children of Israel have lost their way and that the desert has engulfed them. I will (thereby) harden the heart of Pharaoh so that he pursues them." Again, when the sea split before the Hebrews, it was as if by a natural cause, so that the Egyptian army would brave the crossing: "The Lord drove the sea with a powerful east wind all night, drying the sea and splitting the waters."

"It was then that Moses and the Children of Israel sang this song to the Lord saying in effect. . . ." Rather than being a psalm of thanksgiving or a hymn of praise, the Song of the Sea is an anthem celebrating the reentry of Divinity into the world of human affairs. It rejoices with God at His finding it possible to penetrate into a sphere that had been managed by a profane king and civilization.

Divinity's return into His creatures' history came in the wake of the conflict between the Egyptians and the Hebrews. God heard, saw, and knew what was necessary in order to save the Hebrew victim from oppression. God is pictured as following a model prefigured by Moses when he found an Egyptian beating a Hebrew. Moses the Hebrew foundling had been raised as an Egyptian prince, and he was free to choose his identity. He made an irrevocable choice by considering the Hebrew victim his brother and killing the Egyptian. God's actions at the Red Sea conform to this pattern. The Song of the Sea applauds God's moving ahead with His oath to redeem Israel and return her to her homeland. Thus, the song ends with, "You bring and plant him (Israel) on Your holy mountain, the place of Your habitation which You O Lord created, this Divine sanctuary which You have fashioned." The lyrics also express their commitment to the Almighty for saving them, as in "The Lord is a warrior whose name is the Lord," but if the song were mainly about military triumphalism, the population of women would not have been singled out as embracing it in dance.

As a prior step in their covenant with God, the People of Israel were required to demonstrate their separation from Egyptian peoplehood and religion. This was enacted through the Passover ritual, God's first commandment to Israel as a nation. Each household was to designate a lamb for slaughter and hold it four days for the Egyptians to see. Moses had remarked to Pharaoh early on, "Could we slaughter the deities of the Egyptians before their eyes without them stoning us!" Thus shocking the natives, the Israelites were to sacrifice thousands of lambs on the eve of the 14 of Nissan and display the lamb's blood on the doorposts. Showing further contempt for the Egyptian religion, they were to roast the lamb intact on a spit, then eat it down to the last morsel by morning. Once they rejected the surrounding pagan culture and performed God's ritual, He led them out of Egypt. "And you shall tell your son on that day, saying, 'It is because of this that the Lord favored me when he took me out of Egypt'" (13:8).

Defeating the pursuing Egyptian army is not remarkable for the Omnipotent but choosing the People of Israel is. At the crossing of the Red Sea we have a mutual commitment between the Divine and Israel, a commitment that King Solomon would depict in his Song of Songs as a marriage. The problems that are soon to intrude on this new relationship are best understood as the expected surprises and adjustments which new partnerships experience.

The name for Divinity projected in this relationship is the Tetragrammaton, the Lord, the Divine's 4-letter personal aspect. But in a brief interlude between the redemption from Egypt and the revelation at the Red Sea, the formal name "God" (Elohim) is used four times in a row: "When Pharaoh let the people go, God did not lead them by way of the Philistine land – the short route – because God thought that perhaps the people will feel regret upon facing war and return to Egypt. . . ." Here we are shown a universal aspect of Divinity, which takes into account natural causes and human nature. This usage puts into sharp contrast the personal quality of the Lord projected in freeing Israel from slavery, in rescuing them at the Red Sea, and in the developing relationship.

The relationship gets off to a bad start, with the people complaining to Moses about conditions in the desert and Moses telling God that if things get any worse the people might stone him. In response to the atmosphere of confusion, God introduces the Sabbath and the Manna. The Sabbath had not been mentioned since God Himself sanctified the seventh day at creation. Here God grants Israel His Sabbath. But humans also need food and God provides Manna, a gift falling from heaven above.

That the granting of the Manna and the Sabbath has symbolic meaning is indicated by the text's breaking out of its time frame, to past and future. Mention is made that the Israelites will live on Manna for the next forty years, "until they reach settled land," and of course the Sabbath draws us to the beginning of time.

The Israelites move on to Rephidim, and this move signals that the giving of the Torah at Sinai is on the horizon, because Rephidim will be mentioned again as being the last stop before Mount Sinai. When the people here complain of thirst, Moses is instructed to go to Horeb, another name for Sinai, and strike the rock to start a flow of water from "the mountain of God." Again in Rephidim, Amalek attacks and God blesses Israel's armed resistance. Again near the mountain of God, Jethro the father-in-law of Moses comes from Midian, and reunites Moses with his wife and children. After a celebration, Moses receives advice from his father-in-law on how to reduce the stream of persons who request the word of God from Moses. Jethro advises that a formal system be set up with judges to handle the bulk of the cases. Moses accepts the advice, sets up a court system, then "Moses sent off his father-in-law, who returned to his land." A parallel account in Numbers 10:29 shows Moses pleading with his father-in-law not to leave but stay and enjoy the good God has promised Israel. It seems that the point of the Exodus account is that outsiders, no matter how wise and loving, have no place in the Sinai convocation which follows. Similarly, the engagement with Amalek prior to Sinai underscores that both friend and enemy must be kept at a distance before Israel can achieve the lonely stance needed for receiving the Torah.

But the giving of the Ten Commandments and the Torah was not the central occurrence of the Sinai revelation. Rather it was the formal sealing of the bond between God and Israel, with formal declarations of expectations and conditions by the parties: "'Now, if you obey Me and uphold My covenant, then you shall be My choice from among the peoples – since the whole world is Mine – and you shall be My nation of priests and a holy people....' All the people responded in unison, 'We will do whatever the Lord says.'"

Moses is again the go-between and God accords him individual recognition, "When the people hear Me addressing you, they will always believe in you as well." Moses tells the people, "Prepare yourselves for three days; do not approach a woman for intimacy." But God had told him only to have them prepare for the third day without the mention of women. It seems that the Torah prefers to have a man talk to the men in this way, whereas God is shown addressing the men and women equally. Along the same lines, the caption on the last of the Ten Commandments is, "Do not covet your friend's home," while Moses, as a male, repeats the caption in Deuteronomy 5:18 as "Do not covet your friend's wife."

When God tells Moses to go down from the mountain and warn the people not to advance for a glimpse of Divinity, Moses demonstrates his characteristic strong-mindedness by saying that it isn't necessary for him to descend since he already did convey God's warning. God's response, "Go down and then come up, you and Aaron with you," seems a rebuke identical to the one hurled at Moses from the burning bush: "Aaron too shall share in your glory."

Having addressed the Ten Commandments to the entire nation, God then provides Moses with further explanations, including an overview of the Divine law code, to accompany the covenant. That it is a brief characterization of the tenor of Divine justice, with specifics to follow, is indicated by phrases such as, "I will arrange for a place where the killer can escape to," referring to future cities in which an unintentional killer can find refuge.

The code begins with substantive law, such as, "When you buy a Hebrew slave, he is to work six years and go free on the seventh." It moves on to procedural law, such as, "Do not pervert the justice of the poor.... Do not accept bribes.... Do not favor the weak in a lawsuit." It moves on to social justice, "Do not mistreat the stranger, for you know how a stranger feels...." It mentions the Sabbath and holidays, then urges sensitivity to diet and to the animal world, "Do not cook a kid in its mother's milk." It returns to the theme of being loyal to God, and that God will plant Israel securely in the entire Holy Land, "from the Sea of Reeds to the Philistine sea, and from the desert to the river."

Moses then came down from the mountain and presented all of the above to the people, and again they said yes. The next day, Moses committed the agreement to writing, including in this Book of the Covenant all the conditions, understandings, laws, and commandments which we read in the text from Israel's arrival at the foot of Sinai. Then Moses built a sacrificial altar, sprinkled half of the sacrificial blood over the crowd, and read out the agreement, to which the crowd responded, "Whatever the Lord said we shall do and obey." Then Moses went back up the mountain to spend the next forty days receiving the rest of the commandments, the Torah, and the Tablets of Stone.

Surprisingly, our text presents the structure of the Tabernacle, and the design of the priestly vestments, as the subject of the Divine instructions to Moses. God also provided Moses with a visual image, "As I show you this structure of the Tabernacle and of its implements, so shall you make it." Again, "As you were shown on the mountain, so shall they construct it" (27:8). This last verse may refer to the mystical vision in 24:10, "They witnessed the God of Israel, under whose feet was a structure of sapphire brick as pure as the essence of heaven." This vision, seen by Moses, Aaron, Nadav, Avihu, the seventy elders and their functionaries, provided a glimpse of the future Tabernacle, seen as the structure on which the Divine glory stood, that kabbalists term "the Divine Chariot." This term is applied primarily to the mystical vision in Ezekiel, and the wording at the end of the first chapter of Ezekiel mirrors the language of the Sinaitic vision.

Still, the nation of Israel waiting at the foot of the mountain is central to the instructions about the Tabernacle. Firstly, the nation is declared to be God's proxy for receiving the materials needed for building, in that donations accepted by the national unit are seen as accepted by God. Secondly, when in chapter 30 a census is ordered to count the total number of Israelite men, the half shekel that each one gives becomes that individual's share in the Tabernacle. Thirdly, the main purpose of the Tabernacle is to unite Israel with its God: "Have them make Me a sanctuary so I can dwell in their midst." Further, the Divine will be in constant communication with Israel through this sanctuary, "I shall meet you [Moses] there, and I shall speak to you from above the ark cover, from between the two Cherubs which are on the Ark of Testimony, with all that I order you to convey to the Children of Israel" (25:22).

That the purpose of the Tabernacle was to cement the relationship between God and Israel, and not mainly for Israel's sacrifices, is conveyed by the delay in ordering construction of the Golden Altar, the incense altar which was placed inside the Communion Tent. All other implements are commanded in the order of their placement, from the inner sanctum outward. Indeed, in the subsequent half-dozen times that the Tabernacle's implements are listed, the Golden Altar is properly listed just after the Menorah oil lamp. But God's command to build such an inside altar does not come until chapter 30, after all the implements, and even the priestly clothing, are ordered. The point is to avoid having God appear as needing the sacrificial service for Himself, as the popular pagan imagination would have it. Thus the Babylonian Creation Epic pictures the gods creating mankind so that men can provide food for the gods inside temple altars: "Man shall be his name; verily savage-man will I create. He shall be charged with the service of the gods, that they might be at ease." It is such an imagined view of the ritual altar that Isaiah and other prophets rail against, "What need have I of your many sacrifices, says the Lord. I am oversated with ram burnt offerings and animal fat, and I don't want the blood of bulls, sheep, or goats" (1:11).

While the outside altar, in the yard of the Tabernacle, is ordered in its expected architectural slot, it is the inside altar which could have excited imagined mystical purposes and which is played down in God's direct command. Instead, it is the lighting of the Menorah lamp that is the first-mentioned priestly service for a completed Tabernacle, and the lighting of the lamp is the ritual kept in prominence through repetition, as we will see.

Chapter 27 ends, "... ignite a steady lamp. Let Aaron and his sons light it from evening to morning before the Lord in the Tent of Communion, outside the curtain which covers the Ark of Testimony." If the Golden Altar's mention is late, this mention of lighting the lamp is early, since it mentions Aaron as priest although Aaron's selection for the priesthood comes only later, in the next chapter. The lamp service is mentioned twice more at the end of chapter 30, again in Leviticus 24, and again in Numbers 8 – this last in partial contrast to animal sacrifice.

When the inside altar is finally ordered, it is designated for incense only – no animal or meal offerings. It is to be placed "... in front of the curtain which covers the Testament, where I meet with you." This last phrase emphasizes again that the basic reason for a Tabernacle is to bring together God and his servants, not just to service God, even with mere frankincense or light.

Even the ordering of the outside altar, which is designated for animal and meal offerings, hints at sensitivity to the charge – which the prophets will rail against – that Divinity has use of men's gifts. The first sacrifices that God prescribes for the altar are for the ceremonial inauguration of Aaron's priesthood and for the consecration of the altar, not for service to God. Further, this long 46-verse section ends with a reminder of the Tabernacle's central purpose: "The continual sacrifice unto your generations is for the front of the Tent of Communion, before the Lord, where I may meet with you there to speak with you there. I shall meet with the Children of Israel there and it shall be sanctified through My glory" (29:42).

God's instructions on the Tabernacle require over five chapters and are given a closing statement concerning the Sabbath. This is the fifth time that the Sabbath has been mentioned in the Torah, but its observance here ties in with the Tabernacle in that the Sabbath too "is a sign between Me and you for your generations, so that it be known that it is I who sanctifies you" (31:13). The forty days on Mount Sinai coming to an end, God gives Moses the stone tablets inscribed with the Ten Commandments.

Meanwhile below, the people started to worship a Golden Calf, and God reports this to Moses, using the exact words which the narration had already ascribed to the idolaters: "They said, 'These are your gods, O Israel, who have taken you out of Egypt.'" Moses responds with an appeal to God, preventing the immediate destruction of Israel, and he descends to the camp. Upon seeing first hand the worship of the Golden Calf, Moses smashes the Tablets at the foot of the mountain and proceeds to punish the wrongdoers, helped by his Levite brethren. The next day, Moses says to the people, "You have committed a great sin; now let me go up to the Lord and perhaps I can get you forgiveness for your sin" (32:30).

God is pleased with Moses' valiant efforts on behalf of the nation, and in turn Moses uses God's affection for Moses to press for their total forgiveness: "If Your good favor does not accompany us, do not take us from here, for how will it be known that I find favor in Your eyes – both I and Your people – if You do not accompany us, and I and Your people will be distinct from all the people on earth.... Let me kindly see Your glory."

To this last request, Moses receives three answers: yes, no, and this third mystical resolution – "Said the Lord, 'Here is a space near Me where you can stand on the rock, and when My glory approaches I shall place you in the crevice of the rock, then I shall cover you with My palm until I pass. When I remove My palm you may witness My departure but My front may not be seen'" (33:23).

At this point God agrees to reinstate Israel's lapsed covenant. He orders Moses to hew two new stone tablets onto which the Divine will inscribe again the Ten Commandments. Again, Moses is told to ascend the mountain at daybreak, with the original warning being repeated: "Let no man ascend with you and let no man be seen anywhere on the mountain, even sheep and cattle shall not graze at that mountain." God announces again that He and Israel are to be bound by covenant. God repeats for Moses the essentials of the earlier covenant in chapter 23, and now ends again with, "Do not cook a kid in its mother's milk." Moses is told to commit the covenant's text to writing again; then Moses leaves to spend another forty days on Sinai, eating no bread and drinking no water.

It becomes obvious that the sin of the Golden Calf canceled each successive step that had been taken to establish Israel as the Chosen People, and that each step had to be reauthorized and re-enacted. Surprisingly, when Moses finally returns from Mount Sinai – now with an angelic halo – he orders the construction of the Tabernacle. This is surprising because, after the Golden Calf, Moses had not received reauthorization for a sanctuary, the symbol of the unique closeness of God and Israel.

Moses seems aware that he is on unsure ground in having the Tabernacle built. His orders begin with mention of the Sabbath, which God had however placed last, because Moses felt safe in asserting that God's words about the Sabbath were still valid. He proceeds with the specifics of construction using the precise words or paraphrases of God's original instructions. Moses could argue that while the Divine words had not been reauthorized, neither had they been withdrawn. Still, it was on his own authority that Moses prompted Israel to build a sanctuary. Will Moses succeed in this bold initiative, presenting the Divine with a *fait accompli*? And what will be the Divine response? It is the dramatic tension in these questions that accompanies the half-dozen repetitions of the Tabernacle's components, repetitions that the casual reader would have considered superfluous.

In any event, the people responded enthusiastically. So much so that soon they had to curtail the donations, announcing, "Let no man or woman produce anything more as an offering to the sanctuary. So the people stopped bringing."

About halfway through the restating of all the Tabernacle's components, an interruption for bookkeeping puts an end to the suspense of whether or not Moses' project will succeed: "These are the figures for the Tabernacle, the Tabernacle of Testimony, accounted for by Moses and served by the Levites under the control of Ithamar son of Aaron the Priest . . . All the gold used in the construction of all the sacred implements, coming from the offerings of gold, came to 29 talents and 720 shekels. . . ." The text goes on to account for the silver and copper totals as well. This mention of Ithamar pushes the narrative beyond the immediate time frame, since Ithamar was not appointed over the Levites until after the tragic deaths of his elder brothers Nadav and Avihu in Leviticus, by which time the Tabernacle had become a successful reality. The interruption, accounting for the precious metals, serves to defend Moses from any evil-minded suspicions that Moses had anything to gain from initiating this elaborate construction project.

At this point, each of the priestly vestments is described and each description is punctuated with the refrain, "as the Lord *had* commanded Moses." When the finished parts for the Tabernacle were presented to Moses, "Moses inspected the work and, behold, they had made it just as the Lord had commanded it, and Moses blessed them" (39:43). Moses, realizing the precariousness of his initiative, now feels relieved and heartened by the architectural success of the venture. Of course, Moses had been provided with a visual image of the sanctuary during his first forty days on Sinai and now he saw how the finished product was miraculously picture perfect, and, elated, he blessed the workmen.

Finally Divine approval arrives: "The Lord spoke to Moses saying, 'On the first day of the first month assemble the Tabernacle with the Communion Tent . . .'" Moses assembles and services the sanctuary, and the old refrain returns, now to be understood as "as The Lord has (not 'had') commanded Moses."

After Moses completes the sanctuary, "A cloud covered the Tent of Communion and the glory of the Lord filled the Tabernacle. Moses could not enter the Tent of Communion because the cloud rested upon it and the glory of the Lord filled the Tabernacle" (40:34). God's approval and ultimate pleasure over Moses' initiative was so great that the resulting Divine glory was too intense for even the very person who made possible the advent of the Divine glory.

Moses' insistence that there be a sacred space for God's visitations with Israel is foreshadowed early on. During the dark days of Divine wrath that came with the worship of the Golden Calf,

"Moses would take his tent and place it far outside the camp and call it the Communion Tent, so that anyone who sought the Lord would go to the Communion Tent which was outside the camp. . . . And when Moses came to the tent, the Cloud Bank would descend, remain at the tent door, and speak to Moses" (33:7).

PART III

A Guide to the Book of Leviticus

"HE CALLED TO MOSES and the Lord spoke to him from the Tabernacle saying, 'Speak to the Children of Israel and say to them: "If a person offers a sacrifice to the Lord …"'" The next 250 verses in Leviticus deal with the offerings for the Divine altar. These first ten chapters of Leviticus portray Divinity as inviting or commanding animal sacrifice and libations. Such a posture was avoided in the books of Genesis and Exodus. As often as sacrifices are mentioned in these prior books, a direct quote by God demanding devotion through sacrifices is hard to find. Noah's sacrifice after the flood is shown as coming from the worshipper's own initiative, as are the earlier sacrifices of Cain and Abel. The Patriarchs' sacrifices are also pictured as mainly self-initiated, and Abraham's twilight sacrifice in Genesis 15 was triggered by his request for a Divine promise of the gift of the land.

Exodus' Passover lambs were to be eaten entirely by the devotees, and the blood on the doorposts was to save them from the Death of the Firstborn plague. Then the sacrifices at the Covenant of Sinai are shown as on Moses' initiative, with any Divine command omitted. The Divine directive about an altar for animal sacrifice, in Exodus 20, is more an "if" than a demand: "You may make Me a dirt altar for your burnt offerings and peace offerings … and if you would make Me a stone altar, do not hew them.…" Further, the altars for the sanctuary are not presented as the structure's main purpose. Rather, the sanctuary is defined as the sacred space where, "I shall meet you there and tell you from above the cover between the two Cherubs, which are on the Ark of Testimony, all that I command you for the Children of Israel" (Exodus 25:22). Lest one still imagine that not the Ark but the altar is the central implement of the sanctuary, the inside Golden Altar is ordered last, adjoining the outside Wash Basin.

While Exodus 29 has God ordering a long list of sacrifices, these are not for pure worship but for the purpose of consecrating the priesthood and for the initiation of the altar itself. Even here, God repeats that the sanctuary's real function is "where I can commune with you to speak to you. There I shall present Myself to the Children of Israel . . ." (verse 42).

When Moses finally erects the sanctuary, "he placed the sacrificial altar at the entrance of the Communion Tent's Tabernacle, and he offered upon it the burnt offering and the meal offering, as the Lord had commanded Moses" (Exodus 40:29). But in the parallel Divine command, in verse 10, God's request for these sacrifices is studiously omitted.

As powerful a form of worship as these sacrifices are, they invite a problem in actual practice: The worshipper may think of himself as giving God what He wants, and expect that the Omnipotent will return the favor by granting the devotee what he needs and wants. A devotee may approach the sacrificial altar in an effort to manipulate Divinity. Such a crass understanding of animal sacrifice developed in the pagan religions, from the ancient Babylonians to the American Aztecs. Such an attempt at manipulation is evidenced in Numbers 23, where Balaam the Seer dares address God in such terms: "I have set up the seven altars and have sacrificed a bull and a ram on each altar." There is a response to this imagined manipulation in Psalm 50:

Hear this, Israel, the testament of your Almighty God.
I make no demand for your sacrifices,
Your household oxen nor sheepfold rams.
Owning the beasts and animals in mountain forests,
Knowing every bird and creature in the wild,
I don't need your bread – the world is Mine.

I don't eat fatlings nor drink the blood of lamb,
Just bring the Lord your thanksgiving gifts,
And make good on your free-will offerings,
Turn to Me when troubled, then acknowledge when I help.

Chapter one of Isaiah provides an even sharper protest against a misuse of the sacrifice ritual: "'Why do I need your abundant sacrifices?' asks the Lord. 'I am oversated with the ram burnt offerings and the fat of sheep. I did not ask for the blood of bulls, of lambs and goats....'"

But the Book of Leviticus prescribes at length the precise methods of worship for the sacrificial altar. Even so, Leviticus is careful to begin with the voluntary form of such worship, the burnt offerings and the meal offerings. Prescribed next is the peace offering, which has the worshipper share in the major cuts of meat, with only designated internal organs, fat, and blood for the altar.

Next, the sacrifice ritual is expanded to include a response to sin: "If a soul sins by mistake ..." (4:2). Leviticus began by terming the worshipper a "person," but now in connection with sinning the worshipper is termed a "soul." The idea is that God, in His mercy, provides this avenue through which to heal a poor, sick soul, so as to return the soul to its proper state. Thus, the first mentioned example of such a sinner is the high priest, for his soul begs most for a return to pure spirituality.

These sin offerings cover over misdeeds made by mistake, but soon enough the sacrificial ritual is extended to rectify for a sinner who bears a level of guilt, and we are introduced to the guilt offering. The first type of guilt offering groups together a triad of irresponsible behavior: The first against another person, the second against Divinity, and the third against the sinner himself. In the first instance, the sinner neglected or refused to testify in court in someone's defense; in the second, the sinner violated the sanctity of the sanctuary; in the third, he swore an oath but did not honor his own resolution.

If in violating the sanctuary the sinner benefited by the use of a sacred object, he must also make restitution and bring a special guilt offering. There is also a special guilt offering for the "soul" who is not sure whether or not he has sinned, since the resulting turmoil in such a soul also requires repair.

Finally in Leviticus 5:20, a guilt offering is prescribed for out-and-out theft. Here the guilty soul stole something, swore his innocence before God, and then comes seeking penance and restitution. The triad of man, God, and self is repeated here in a single sin.

At this point, there is a return to the beginning of the series starting with the burnt offering and the meal offering, but now the added procedures are addressed to the priesthood: "Command Aaron and his sons as follows. This is the law of the burnt offering …" (6:2). Then, where we expect the laws of the peace offering, there is an interruption for a new requirement, the meal sacrifice which Aaron and every new priest must bring at inauguration. With this interruption, the Book of Leviticus is well on its way to establish the priesthood as being its central concern and establish Aaron as the central figure of its narrative. Thus, if Moses was the human hero of the Book of Exodus, then Aaron is becoming the hero of the Book of Leviticus, as we will see.

The peace offering, which lost its expected slot to Aaron's inauguration sacrifice, is now placed at the end of the list, but here it is addressed instead to all Israel, who are reminded that this sacrifice is optional. Still, should they bring this sacrifice, they must give the priest his portion – the right leg and the breast. A surprising summary mentions Sinai: "This is the law of the burnt, meal, sin, guilt, inaugural, and peace offerings which the Lord commanded Moses on Mount Sinai, on the day which He commanded the Children of Israel to bring their sacrifices to the Lord in the desert of Sinai" (8:37). Of course, much has happened since the initial commandments and the selection of Aaron as the high priest during Moses' forty days on the mountain. For when Israel made the Golden Calf there was a period of doubt about there ever being a sanctuary with its ritual. Aaron's position as high priest was in doubt because of his role in the Golden Calf fiasco, and Moses tells how he had to pray then to save Aaron's life (Deuteronomy 9:20). But the mention of Sinai in the summary, in effect returns Aaron and the sacrifice ritual to the pristine spirituality and to the absolute Divine favor of the original Sinai revelation. This pronouncement then serves as the introduction to the next sixty verses, which describe in meticulous detail an eight-day process through which Aaron and the sanctuary are to be consecrated.

The mention of Sinai here is but the first of four such flashbacks to Mount Sinai in Leviticus, and we will return to this feature again.

On the eighth day of the consecration, a flame leaped out to consume the ready sacrifices on the altar, this fire signaling the Divine acceptance of Israel's worship, and the assembled crowd shouts its praise. But the same flame from God also flashed upon Aaron's sons, Nadav and Avihu, who were performing an unauthorized ritual in the Sanctum, killing them. Amidst the joy and mourning, Moses tries to console the bereaved father. Aaron does not answer. Then God speaks directly to Aaron, ordering that no priest should drink wine before performing the sacred service.

This will be the only time in Leviticus that God addresses Aaron alone with a law of the Torah. Obviously, the revelation here is meant to console, strengthen, and reassure Aaron that his priestly function is wanted. After all, we have here a father who achieves his lifelong dream of personal success but simultaneously loses two of his sons in the effort.

Who is to blame for the tragedy? Moses, who was in charge during the eight days of preparation? No, Moses is shown as having carried out his management duties properly, for the report in chapters 8 and 9 adds the refrain, "as the Lord commanded Moses," repeated five times – the same refrain which signaled perfection at the Tabernacle's erection in Exodus 40.

Still, because the deaths occurred on Moses' watch, the text reasserts Moses' continuing authority through the use of a chiasmus: During the eight-day preparations Moses is quoted as saying variously, "as I ordered – as the Lord ordered – as I was ordered" (chapter 8). Then after the tragedy, we find in chapter 10, "as I was ordered – as the Lord ordered – as I ordered." This ABC-CBA chiastic arrangement reasserts Moses' competence to speak for God both before and after the tragedy.

Aaron too is shown as not to blame for his sons' mistakes, because at the end of chapter ten Aaron is shown as understanding the ritual better than Moses:

Moses inquired about the goat's sin offering and discovered that it had been burnt. He rebuked Elazar and Ithamar, Aaron's surviving sons, saying, "Why did you not eat the sin offering?" Then Aaron answered Moses, "When they sacrificed their sin offering and burnt offering before the Lord today, and this is what happened to me. And if I should eat of a sin offering today would it be good in the eyes of the Lord?" Moses listened and was satisfied.

The sadness of the bereaved high priest and his need for gentle reassurance remain on the agenda for additional chapters in Leviticus. The next new chapter, which sets the laws of Kosher and non-Kosher animals, is addressed to both Moses and Aaron. Indeed, between this chapter 11 and chapter 15 – where the death of Aaron's sons is mentioned explicitly – the Divine expounds the law to Moses and Aaron jointly four times, including the laws of leprosy, the laws of a diseased house, and the laws of bodily purity for men and women. We have here a demonstration of continued concern for the mourning father, who needs to be told that he is wanted and worthy of being the high priest.

After these new laws are promulgated, there is typically a summary statement, for example, "This is the law concerning the animals, the birds, and all living things that swarm the waters ... to distinguish between the impure and the pure ..." (11:46). These summaries are not part of God's speeches to Moses and Aaron but part of the text's comment. It may be necessary to have these statements here to enshrine the Torah law, because together with the legal aspects here there are the concomitant expressions of consolation to Aaron, and the narrative line may have been taken as weakening the legal aspects, if not for the summaries.

Two of the new laws in these chapters are addressed to Moses alone, and these laws begin with a happy note: "When a woman is fruitful and gives birth to a boy ..." (chapter 12); and "This is the law for the leper on the day that he becomes clean ..." (chapter 14). It may be that the celebratory tone in these two situations would have aroused a jarring thought for a father recovering from the death of his two boys. While these situations require Aaron's ministry, they are addressed to Moses.

A thematic, repeated word indicates how essential Aaron the Priest is to these laws, and how central Aaron is to the Book of Leviticus. "The priest looks and sees," occurs some forty times in these chapters. We have noted how "seeing" is a thematic word in Genesis with the singular expression, "He raised his eyes and saw," and in Exodus where "seeing" occurs repeatedly at Moses' birth, at the burning bush, at Sinai, and in "God heard, saw, and knew." So the Book of Leviticus too features "seeing" as a thematic word, appropriately attaching it to a priest's sight, for the priesthood and Aaron are the focus of Leviticus from the start, in both the legislative and narrative sense.

The introduction to chapter 16 brings up Aaron's tragedy once more: "The Lord spoke to Moses after the deaths of Aaron's two sons. . . ." What follows is the Yom Kippur service, the longest and most intricate of any ritual passage in Leviticus. Still, the articulation of the ritual prescription stays in touch with the narrative introduction. For instance, verse 12 begins, "Let [Aaron] take a pan filled with fiery coals from the altar before the Lord, and handfuls of powdered incense, to bring in beyond the curtain. Let him place the incense on the fire before the Lord, and the smoke of incense shall cloud over the cover of the Testament, and he will not die." The language here is reminiscent of Nadav and Avihu's tragic worship, with the words "take," "pan," "place," "fire," "incense," "before the Lord," and "die," appearing in both instances. By then Aaron was ready to confront his sons' mistaken worship and to accept Moses' assurance that he will not die doing the comparable incense service. It is remarkable that even in commanding the ritual for the year's holiest day, the Torah includes an awareness of the human feelings involved.

The next chapter continues along these lines: "Let the Children of Israel, who sacrifice out in the fields, bring them rather to the Lord, to the gate of the Tabernacle, to the priest, so as to sacrifice them as peace offerings to the Lord . . . so that they will no longer sacrifice their sacrifices to the ghosts, after whom they scamp . . ." (17:5). This mention of their whoring after ghost spirits seems like a gratuitous slap at Israel's practice. But again, since this chapter is addressed primarily to Aaron as priest (verse 2), it amounts to an encouragement to Aaron. It again says to Aaron that he is wanted, and needed, to save Israel form a degrading ritual, because he and his sons will be there to administer the Divine worship.

Chapter eighteen introduces a refrain that will reoccur through the next six chapters: "I am the Lord your God." These chapters will provide for increasing purity and holiness, at first for the nation and then for the priesthood. To begin, the Torah prohibits incest and lists the other prohibited marriages. At one point, a prohibition against offering one's children to the fires of Molech intrudes into the list: "Do not inject your semen for offspring into another's wife, in defilement. And do not present your children to pass them by Molech … and do not lie with a male as with a woman, this an abomination …" (18:20). This intrusion of Molech worship here points to the notion that when a child is born from an unlawful union, the unwanted child may be selected by the parents to sacrifice to Molech, either out of shame or out of an attempt at forgiveness. Thus, the sin of Molech is placed in the list after the cases of adultery that can produce a child and before those that cannot produce a child, the cases of homosexuality and bestiality that follow.

From chapter nineteen, a new refrain is added: "Be holy for I am Holy." This refrain provides the theme behind Leviticus' ritual laws, going back to the book's early rules, such as the Kosher law (20:25) and behind the new rules about loving your neighbor – even a stranger – as yourself, in what amounts to an elaboration and extension of the Ten Commandments.

The twenty-first chapter turns to the special holiness expected of the priests. They are to limit their contact with the dead and participate only in the funerals of their close relatives. A priest may not marry a divorcee, while the high priest may only marry a virgin and may not participate in the funeral of even his father or mother. In order to take part in the sanctuary service, a priest must be without blemish or injury, and only an unblemished animal may be sacrificed in the holy ritual.

This mention of the sacrificial animal elicits a tone of sympathy for animals: "When a calf, sheep, or goat is born, let it stay with its mother for seven days. … And do not slaughter a cow or sheep and its son on the same day ..." (22:27). The mention of mother and son is certain to win empathy for the animal species and to foster recognition of the maternal instinct in animals.

Yet another aspect of holiness is introduced in chapter twenty-three, sacred time and the holidays: "These are the Lord's holidays which you are to proclaim as holy festivals, these are My holidays. For six days shall you do labor, but the seventh day is a Sabbath for rest, do not labor...." The surprising intrusion of the Sabbath into the list of holidays underscores that the idea of there being sanctity of time is being established here. The Sabbath is placed at the head of the holiday list because the Sabbath is the root of the phenomenon of sacred time, that a moment of ongoing time can be more holy than another. The seventh day of creation, the Sabbath, initiated the concept of sacred time, and as Leviticus goes about naming the holidays it suggests that Sabbath's holiness is the source of each festival's holiness. Thus Yom Kippur, Rosh Hashana, and Succoth are termed Sabbaths, as indeed the term "Sabbath" is given an extended meaning, with the word "Sabbath" occurring over a dozen times in this chapter. By contrast, the presentation of the holidays in the 28th chapter of the Book of Numbers does not repeat Sabbath even once, outside its use with the Sabbath proper. This is why the Jewish tradition is able to understand the verse, "Count for yourselves from the day after the Sabbath ..." (23:15), as referring to the holiday-Sabbath of Passover, whereas other traditions take it to mean a Sunday. The Jewish traditional reading is rooted in the Leviticus context, with its broad usage for the term Sabbath, a reading that would not have been possible in the Numbers or Deuteronomy contexts, with their different emphases in rendering the holidays.

The first and main part of Leviticus is about to end, and what follows here serves to bring it to a close: "Command the Children of Israel to bring you pure olive oil, pressed for illumination to light a constant lamp, placed outside the curtain of testament in the Tabernacle. Let Aaron set it before the Lord from evening to morning constantly ..." (24:2). These words are a repeat of Exodus 27:20, where it constitutes the very first service with which Aaron was charged. But here in its Leviticus setting, "constant" appears four times. It reflects on Aaron's new frame of mind, after his heartbreak and hesitation, to now being capable of a steady, constant service. This is in contrast with his frame of mind after his sons' deaths, when even in the Yom Kippur service he was reassured that "only once a year" would he be engaged in a service that robbed him of sons. In addition, here the lamp is termed "the *pure* Menorah," with the adjoining command about the showbreads using the term "the *pure* table" twice more. For at this point in the book's campaign for purity and holiness, Aaron's service can be characterized as both pure and steady. The law for the holiness ends with, "Let Aaron and his sons eat it in a holy place, because holy of holiness is right for him, from the Lord's offerings, forever" (24:9), this closing line having the flavor of a gift of appreciation for Aaron's brave loyalty and service.

Suddenly there enters a jarring episode about blasphemy. But this episode also serves as closure for the first part of Leviticus. The blasphemy incident provides us with an additional understanding of holiness by having us look at the opposite side of the coin, with holiness' other extreme, with the degradation against which holiness must contend. As such, the incident of blasphemy contributes to the summary close of the book's campaign for holiness. In addition, it contributes closure to the narrative of Aaron's struggle to remain the leader of worship after his son's deaths in the Tabernacle. It hints to us that if Aaron had not been able to accept God's punishment with silence – "Aaron was silent" (10:3) – there loomed before him a possible blasphemy.

In the present incident, the blasphemer was the son of an Egyptian father, and thus missing the sanctity, which is Leviticus' goal. The blasphemer remains nameless, as does the Egyptian father and even the Hebrew man who clashed with the blasphemer. But his mother, Shelomith bat Divri of Dan, is named, as if to say that she and her tribe are blameless. The blasphemer himself is called a stranger or convert, but the text is careful not to turn the incident into a source of hate for strangers: The dispute is framed as between "the son of an Israelite woman and an Israelite man," instead of between an Egyptian convert and an Israelite man. Verse 22 reaffirms, "You are to have one and the same law for both the stranger and the citizen." Indeed, fairness for the stranger is mentioned some ten times throughout Leviticus. And lest the Divine sentence of execution be seen as self-serving, execution is mentioned for a violation of human life as well. Even the killing of an animal is mentioned as requiring just retribution of sorts.

The 25th chapter begins, "The Lord spoke to Moses at Mount Sinai saying...." Why this break in the chronological development with this flashback to the revelations on Sinai, after the very first verse of Leviticus moves us beyond Sinai to the revelations in the finished Tabernacle? The answer may relate to the intertwining of the book's legislation with the personal account of Aaron's struggle to persevere in the priesthood. The extensive treatment of one person's feelings might detract from the book's impact as Divine text and as a reflection of transcendent wisdom. The incorporation of Sinai's status saves Leviticus from an imagined shortcoming and lets it retain the tone of a timeless text, alongside the other four Books of Moses. Indeed, the anachronistic reference to Mount Sinai, starting as early as chapter seven, appears in the book four times.

The 25th chapter laws have a new setting as well: the Promised Land instead of the desert. Still, early Leviticus did include some laws restricted to the future arrival in the Holy Land, such as the law of the Leprous House and the bringing of the First Fruits. But this chapter does continue the rhetoric established earlier in Leviticus' treatment of the holidays, where the Sabbath is given an extended meaning. Now the Torah legislates a year of rest for the soil and terms it a Sabbath Year. The word "Sabbath" is employed nine times in the chapter's first eight verses. Its use is continued in the next law, the law of the Jubilee Year, designated as the fiftieth year after a count of seven Sabbath Years.

This chapter, which opens with the ownership and husbandry of settled lands, gradually slips downward toward successive worsening scenarios: what to do when one's field is sold off, when his home is sold, when he is short of money and must borrow, when he sells himself into slavery, when the slave owner is a proselyte or pagan. Then ten brief verses assure that all will be well "if you obey My commandments," but are followed by over thirty verses warning of a horrible life and expulsion "if you do not obey Me." The horrors are pronounced with homey precision: Ten women will bake their bread in one oven; and you will be eating the flesh of your sons and daughters. Still, the warning uses rhetoric and scenes familiar in prior sections of Leviticus: A full-seven of sins will garner full-seven of punishment, based on the fullness of seven for the oft-mentioned Sabbath. Further, "Then shall the land makeup for its Sabbaths, during the period of devastation while you are in enemy lands, then shall the land rest and claim her Sabbaths" (36:34).

The warning's last verse comes with a surprise: "These are the commandments, the judgments, and the laws which the Lord set between Himself and the Children of Israel at Mount Sinai through Moses" (verse 46). In other words, the dire warning turns out to be the Book of the Covenant from Sinai, where in Exodus 24:7 we have Moses reading out the agreement that commits the people and God to each other. Omitted in the Exodus account, the text of the covenant finds expression here – the word "covenant" occurs six times in the warning – and again serves to tie Leviticus to Sinai's revelation.

Leviticus draws to a close in the 27th chapter, which begins, "If a man makes a declaration pledging the value of life unto the Lord, then your evaluation shall be fifty sacred shekels for a man twenty to sixty years of age. . . ." The evaluation for a woman, a child, or a senior is also given. In a sense, these closing laws signal the success of Leviticus' program for perfect devotion to God. If the book began with an animal being offered on the Divine altar, here the worshipper conceives of devoting his whole being, his life's value, to God. The text moves on to regulating material donations. At every step in the process, the priest does the evaluation and performs the sacred service – the word "*Cohen*" appearing some ten times. Also here, in line with the book's early theme, is the phrase, "sacred unto the Lord." And the book's closing line reads, "These are the rules which the Lord commanded Moses for the Children of Israel on Mount Sinai." While technically the reference to Mount Sinai is limited to the book's last three chapters, it refers to and reflects on the entire volume in a thematic sense. For one expects just such a sentence to signal that the book has ended, and the adjoining Book of Numbers features such a closing formula in its final sentence as well.

PART IV

Explaining the Book of Numbers

THE BOOK BEGINS IN the desert with a Divine command to take a head count of the Children of Israel. The count, as its elaborate guidelines will show, conveys that each individual counts because he is part of a nation that is precious to God. The census is to be broken down by tribe, and the name of each tribe's leader is listed. These princely names will be repeated three more times – once when a tribe is assigned its place in the four-camp arrangement (chapter 4), once again when these princes donate to the Tabernacle (chapter 7), and a third time when the tribes begin an orderly departure for the Promised Land. Also presented more than once are the census figures and the varied articles donated by the princes. It becomes obvious that there is no concern for brevity at the book's beginning.

The narrative builds on successive commandments to Moses, instead of being moved by happenings, for we have here a demonstration of God's affection for Israel. With its numerous restatements, the presentation reminds us of the conversation in Exodus 32:32, where Moses asks God to forgive Israel for the sin of the Golden Calf "'otherwise erase me from the book which You have written.' Said the Lord to Moses, 'Only one who has sinned to Me shall I erase from My book.'" The amount of space allotted to the Children of Israel in the Book of Numbers documents God's friendship.

This book also gives extended coverage to the tribe of Levi. Thus, if the Book of Leviticus centers on the priesthood and Aaron the Priest, the Book of Numbers deals at length with the Levites. The very first chapter notes how the tribe of Levi was not counted together with the others, but from the age of one month instead of the usual draft age. Thereafter, Numbers devotes some 180 verses to the Levites, with over a dozen separate mentions, whereas Leviticus has just one brief mention (Leviticus 25:32).

If the main theme at Numbers' beginning is God's appreciation of Israel, then the concentration on the Levites is due to the Levites being closely associated with the regular citizenry, whereas the priests have an elite sacred aura. The Levites represent all Israel for the service in the Tabernacle, through which God stays in touch with the nation. In addition, the Levites are shown to be replacements for the whole nation's firstborns (3:12), so that the Levite service represents the entire people.

Still, the priests are not overlooked and are listed by name (3:1). However, they are listed as they appeared in the past, at Mount Sinai before the deaths of Nadav and Avihu, because Numbers primarily treats the Levite service. The Levites are presented both to the priests as helpers in their sacred work and to the citizenry as their representatives.

The tribe of Levi lists three families, Gershon – the firstborn – Kehoth, and Merori; and they are listed in this order of seniority during the initial census, which included month-old boys and up. However, a second census, which includes the men ages 30 to 50, lists the Kehoth family first because Kehoth was assigned to the holiest parts of the sanctuary, including the Ark of Testimony. Thus, God's favorable attention to the nation stems from its ongoing worship. God's pleasure with Israel's worship is punctuated by the refrain, "The Children of Israel did as God commanded them through Moses," and will culminate with the priestly blessings and with God showering His own blessings on the nation (6:27).

Chapter 5 interrupts this picture-perfect setting with a dose of reality: "Send out of the camp anyone who has leprosy, or a chronic carnal emission, or who touched the dead. Both man or woman, send outside the camp so that they do not sully your encampment where I dwell in their midst. . . ." This interruption extends to dealing at length with three representative cases which may disturb a harmonious community.

Community life may be disturbed by a cheat who steals and brazenly swears his innocence. Should such a person suddenly have a change of heart, he is provided by the Torah with a program through which he can attain acceptance by man and God. The robbery is to be returned, increased by a fifth as penalty, and a guilt offering is brought to the sanctuary. Further, if the cheated person or his heir cannot be found, then the thief makes payment to a priest. Thus, the priesthood, the sacred altar, and full restitution are part of this ritual helping the erstwhile criminal personality to return to the community.

A community may also be disturbed by troubles within a family, and this second case is about a husband who suspects his wife of cheating. Here too the Torah provides a ritual whereby a marriage can be saved, where there was no adultery but rather distrust or misunderstanding. The husband is to bring his wife to the priest who will read out a terrible curse warning of any infidelity and let her drink a dread potion containing God's name and a scoop of dirt from the sanctuary ground. If this bitter water does not execute her, she is declared innocent and can return happily to family life.

The third problematic situation treated here involves the troubled individual himself. Perhaps he was overcome by depression, by seeing no purpose in life, or by fearing a lack of self-control. If and when he miraculously gets a grip on himself and resolves to be rid of his morbidity, then the Torah prescribes an elaborate Nazirite ritual. He declares himself a pious ascetic before God, so that for a set time he will drink no wine, will not cut his hair, and will have no contact with death. If he inadvertently breaks his strict vow, having touched a dead body, he will begin the Nazirite period all over again after doing penance. If he succeeds in completing his period of devotion, he presents his new, self-confident, real self to the priest, who will put him through an elaborate ceremony, with sacrificial offerings, with the priest sharing in a sacred meal, and with the priest shaving and burning the Nazirite's hair. Elevated by the ritual and strengthened by having kept his resolution, the

Nazirite is told to go ahead and drink wine and be like any self-respecting member of the community.

It is at this point that the Torah places the priestly blessings, the words having special meaning coming after an awareness of the problems that may challenge the nation's tranquility:

> May the Lord bless you and keep you,
> May the Lord smile upon you and give you grace,
> May the Lord turn to you and grant you peace.

The elaboration of the three problem types was preceded by the command to send out of the camp the leper, a person with chronic carnal emissions, and any person who touched a corpse. These three may correspond to the three types of community problems treated, with the leper alluding to the criminal personality who should be kept away from his fellow men, with the persons having a chronic carnal emission alluding to the troubled marriage – where the warring couple would also be unable to consummate their marriage – and with the person defiled by death alluding to the Nazirite who must avoid the funeral even of a dear parent.

Chapter 7 finds the now cleansed Chosen People at peace in the worship of God: "On the day that Moses completed the Tabernacle ... the princes of Israel, those who headed the families and conducted their census, brought forth their contributions to the Lord." What follows is the lengthiest episode in the book – 88 verses – recording with precise repetition the identical gifts of each prince. The repetition is meant to accord equal honor to each donor and to demonstrate the peaceful orderliness of the nation via its leadership in devotion to God. However the concluding 89th verse reads: "Whenever Moses entered the sanctuary to speak with Him, he heard the voice speaking to him from atop the cover on the Ark, from between the two Cherubs, and he spoke to him."

This interjection reminds us that mere mortals, even these princes, cannot think of themselves as giving gifts to the Divine and that the true purpose of the sanctuary is to provide a space that brings man before God and where God will communicate with man.

The very next communication builds on this idea: "The Lord spoke to Moses saying: 'Speak to Aaron telling him that when he lights the lamp he should turn the seven lights to shine toward the face of the lamp'" (chapter 8). Aaron's simple service is being paralleled but also contrasted with the sumptuous offerings of the twelve princes. Aaron's providing basic light is placed in contrast to the voluntary sacrifices of generous men. Further, even Aaron's light is not defined as needed illumination for the smooth function of the sanctuary interior; rather, Aaron's service provides the light for the sacred lamp itself, because the esthetics of the sanctuary requires a lamp which is lit, not dark. Aaron creates holy space, while the princes contribute gifts.

The nature of Aaron's service is next extended to the service of the Levites, which, unlike the contributions of the princes, is essential. Special appreciation for their service is underscored here by enlisting 25-year olds, not only 30-year olds and up, as before, and for their service to continue after the age of 50 as assistants to the primary work force.

God's satisfaction with Israel's worship was such that He authorized a Passover celebration on the anniversary of the one celebrated in Egypt. The nation understood that this Passover in the wilderness was a reaffirmation of their faith and freedom. Consequently, a number of persons who were ritually impure and would not be able to participate complained that they were being left out of an event that touched on their very identities. Moses and Aaron conveyed their dismay to God. God's response makes no mention of the complaint, and only indirectly satisfies the petitioners. The response was directed to the nation and for all times. It promulgated a month-later celebration of Passover for anyone who was on a trip away from the sanctuary or who was ritually impure; then added that any person who neglected the Passover out of spite would be cut off from the nation. Thus indirectly, the passions that moved the impure persons to complain were affirmed.

This affirmation is then turned into what is the most drawn-out section in a book which regularly employs repetition to advantage: "On the day that the sanctuary was completed, the cloud covered the sanctuary, and its Tent of Testimony, then at night it became fire-like until morning. So it would always be, the cloud covering it turning fire-like by night. And whenever the cloud lifted off the tent, the Children of Israel would move, and wherever the cloud settled, there the Children of Israel camped. It was by the Lord's order that the Children of Israel traveled and by the Lord's order that they camped, camping as many days as the cloud stayed. Even when the cloud stayed upon the sanctuary for many days the Children of Israel observed the Lord's directive and did not move. Sometimes the cloud would be above the sanctuary for just a few days – still, it was by the Lord's orders that the Children of Israel traveled and by the Lord's orders that they camped. Sometimes the cloud would be there only from evening to daybreak, so that when the cloud rose in the morning they traveled, or after a day and a night, then they traveled. Or a couple of days or a month or a year, as long as the cloud rested atop the sanctuary the Children of Israel stayed and did not move until it rose up for them to move. It was by the Lord's order that they camped and by the Lord's order that they traveled, observing the Lord's directives, the word of the Lord through Moses" (9:15).

Chapter 10 introduces a practical aspect of these journeys, the use of trumpets to announce travel maneuvers and to signal periods of festivities in the camp. In a combination of both the poetic and realistic impulses, Moses turns to his Midianite brother-in-law, or father-in-law, informs him that Israel is departing immediately for the Promised Land, and invites him to join in the goodness that God has prepared for Israel. Moses is pictured as so full of confidence for the future that he cannot contain himself but must let this joy spill over onto those he loves. The word "good" is used in his speech five times over.

Israel departs; then Moses addresses God in two verses which are placed in parentheses, then all the good turns to evil: "The people complained evilly toward the Lord, who took note, became angry, and let loose a Divine flame against the people ..." (11:1). The word "bad" appears some five times whereas before we had "good." What happened? Indeed, from this eleventh chapter through chapter 18 we read of one trouble after another. What happened to the perfect relationship between God and Israel that preceded this?

Toward a response, we come to realize that the organizing principle in the Book of Numbers is not chronology, but successive, simultaneous, and sometimes opposite perspectives of events. At first, Numbers describes how blessed was Israel's desert experience by grouping together all the "good," then it describes how harrowing an experience it was by grouping together all the "bad." The switch is signaled by the two verses in parentheses: "As the Ark journeyed forth Moses declared: 'Arise O Lord so that Your enemies are scattered and Your opponents retreat before You.' Then when encamping Moses would say: 'Dwell O Lord amidst the myriad thousands of Israel'" (10:35).

These two verses, read by themselves, have Moses speaking to his God as if they were partners. The gulf between the human and the Divine is absent. All the "good" at Numbers' beginning, with its idyllic relationship between man and God reached the limits of the partners' separate natures. Portrayed here perhaps is man's love of God without a parallel fear of God, at which point the relationship totters. Such a prospect triggered the switch from the "good" perspective to the "bad" perspective in the continuous narrative.

The next troublesome event has the mixed multitude crying: "We want meat! We remember the fish we ate for free in Egypt, with cucumbers, melons, leeks, onions, and garlic. But now we have no appetite, getting only this Manna" (11:4). The narration quickly debunks their complaint by praising the Manna: "Manna was like sparkling coriander seed, which the people gathered, crushed or milled, cooking it to give it the taste of rich pastry loaves."

But the people's crying was too much for Moses: "Said Moses to the Lord: 'Why did You condemn me by handing me the problems of this entire nation? . . . If You are going to go on doing this to me, please just kill me so that I not witness my own ruin.'"

God's response was for 70 elders to join in Moses' holy spirit and his leadership. But even this solution ran into trouble, when two of the 70 did not come meet with Moses but became prophets nonetheless, which upset Joshua, who then had words with Moses his master.

Meanwhile the promised meat reached the camp in the form of quail, the birds hovering two feet deep around the camp. Even this accommodation did not succeed, for when the people reacted to the providential meal with ugly gluttony, God's punishment was swift.

The next crisis touched on Moses' own marriage, when sister Miriam and brother Aaron expressed hushed criticism of how Moses treated his wife. The narration comes to Moses' defense, calling him the most humble man on earth, and God Himself rebukes Miriam and Aaron, and then punishes Miriam with leprosy. Aaron and Moses pray for Miriam, and the Israelites would not journey for seven days, until Miriam was rehabilitated.

In this considerateness for Miriam we detect a moderation in the string of crises, but the most treacherous trouble to engulf Israel loomed next, with the sending of spies to the Promised Land. The spies are termed princes of the tribes, but they are not the same twelve princes named earlier and listed four times. These were younger leaders, maybe somewhat athletic and up to the rigors of espionage. They returned with a negative report, first saying that the land was good but well fortified, next saying that we are no match for the mighty inhabitants, then saying that the land had a poisonous environment, and finally saying that it was occupied by giants who made the spies feel as small as insects. The increasingly negative statements devastated the Israelite masses, who declared, "Let us appoint a captain and return to Egypt." Two of the spies, Joshua and Caleb, opposed the mass hysteria and were threatened by a mob, before God appeared to Moses to say: "How long shall this nation antagonize Me ... Let Me destroy it with a plague and build you up as a nation greater than it."

Moses prayed for the nation, using a restatement of the Thirteen Qualities of Divine Mercy which God had revealed to Moses at Mount Sinai after the sin of the Golden Calf, at which time God had also threatened to destroy the nation and save only Moses for future peoplehood.

God again forgives, but does not forget. The recognition of Divinity's essence requires that human beings revere His presence. When God in His goodness is willing to deal with His creatures, they must not be misled to imagine Him less than absolute transcendence. The principle that such an insult requires punishment is often demonstrated in Numbers. The punishment here was for

Israel to stay in the wilderness for forty years – corresponding to the forty days of failed espionage, for a death sentence for the ten faithless spies, and for the defeat of the troops that headed for Canaan prematurely against Moses' order.

Punishment having been meted out, God turns to reconciling with the nation, using a series of new commandments. The first: "When you arrive in the homeland which I am presenting to you and you offer an animal sacrifice to the Lord" then the worshiper must add a grain offering and a wine libation (chapter 15). This opening assures the saddened desert dwellers that the nation will eventually get to the Promised Land. Further, the additions to the sacrificial code hint that God will now welcome their worship. The added prescription is spelled out in sixteen calm verses, using the fullness of expression reminiscent of the drawn-out "good" sections of the book. Also added is that any new convert to Israel will be included in the additional requirements because there is to be one and the same law for citizen and proselyte, hinting again that the Israelites may feel as guiltless as any newcomer, who had no part in the sin of the spies.

A second revelation begins, "When you enter the land to which I bring you and you eat of the bread of the land, separate a portion for the Lord ..." (15:17). Here again is the striking mention of Israel's entry to the land, to eat its produce instead of the Manna, which they had insulted.

Next comes consolation via a mention that a repeat of sinning is known to be possible, but that sinning does not necessarily herald doom: "If by mistake you negate all these commandments – all that the Lord commanded you through Moses from beginning to end – when the community was blindly mistaken, then let the united community offer a young bullock for a burnt offering ... so that there will be forgiveness for the whole community of the Children of Israel and for the stranger who lives with them, since the community just made a mistake. Or if a single person errs ... he will be forgiven ... But when a person sins brazenly, he indeed blasphemes and shall be cut off from his people ..." (15:22).

This warning against brazen sinning, invites a story about someone who desecrated the Sabbath, by way of illustration: "In the desert, the Children of Israel saw a man gathering wood on the

Sabbath day ... The Lord said to Moses: 'Have the man executed by stoning ...' The community took him out and stoned him ... as the Lord had commanded Moses (15:32). Thus, we get here both the tone of reconciliation and the tone of warning against any repeat of disobedience to God.

Next, the text sets down the commandment of Tzitzith, the tassels which the men were to knot onto the four corners of their garments. How this new commandment advances the ongoing theme is not spelled out. Perhaps the royal-blue fringe reminds the Israelites that they are royal somebodies, toward negating how the spies saw themselves as insect nobodies. Perhaps the line, "so that you do not scout after your hearts and eyes, which you stray after," reminds us of the spies' misadventure.

In any event, a new crisis surfaces, this a rebellion by Korach, a Levite, against the leadership of Moses and Aaron, saying to them, "Enough, the people are all holy and the Lord dwells in their midst, so why should you lord it over the Lord's community?" (16:3). Korach was supported by 250 clerics and two Reubenite personalities. Together they instigate a mass demonstration near the Tabernacle. The Divine appeared to Moses and Aaron telling them to move away, so that He would destroy the people. Once again Moses prayed for a reprieve, then approached the offenders with peace proposals and with dire warnings. The rebels were unrelenting, and suddenly the earth opened up swallowing Korach's group – as Moses had warned them – and a heavenly flame incinerated the 250 pietists as they were offering incense.

But Korach's rebellion had set off a feeling of disaffection among the masses. They accused Moses and Aaron of complicity, saying, "You have caused the deaths in the Godly nation." Again, God appears in defense of Moses to repeat: "'Get away from these people and I shall destroy them instantly.' Said Moses to Aaron, 'Grab the fire pan, take fire from the altar, ignite the incense and run toward the people to save them' ... Aaron ran amid the people where the plague had already started.... He stood between the dead and the living, so the plague ceased.... Those killed by the plague numbered 14,700" (17:6).

This tragic episode is one of four that brought on a Divine threat of extinction. The first episode was the Golden Calf, where the sin was idolatry and an insult to Divinity. The second episode was triggered by the spies, where the sin constituted an insult to the Holy Land. The third parallel episode was this Korach rebellion, where the sin was an insult to Moses and Aaron. The fourth episode, which will appear in the 25th chapter of Numbers, has the men mixing with Moabite (and Midianite) women, which was a sin against Israel's peoplehood.

In each of these parallel cases there was a threat to end the people but keep Moses; in each case Moses acted to save the people; in each case there was forgiveness but measured punishment; and in each case the number of deaths is cited – as low as 3,000 following the sin of the Golden Calf and rising to 24,000, at the whoring after the Moabite women.

That Korach's rebellion constituted an attack against Aaron's priesthood, beyond the attack on Moses' leadership, is shown by the lengthy treatment which is allotted to solidifying his priestly role. Moses is instructed to collect inscribed walking canes from the twelve tribal princes, with Aaron's signed staff among them, and to place the cane collection in the sanctuary. By morning, Aaron's cane had miraculously blossomed with ripe almonds – a sign from God of Aaron's selection. Then, God speaks directly to Aaron three times in a row, a distinction not replicated elsewhere for Aaron. As if to contradict the slur against Aaron, God declares: "All the sacred offerings which the Children of Israel bequeath to the Lord, I give to you and your sons and daughters, forever and ever" (18:18).

Alongside the largesse to Aaron the Priest, is the mention that the tithes are to go to the tribe of Levi: "I grant all the tithes of the Children of Israel as a bequest to the Levites, in exchange for the work which they do in the Tabernacle, and let the Children of Israel no longer trespass into the Tabernacle to die of sin" (18:21). This gift to the Levites has reference to Korach's sin, for he was a Levite and should have been satisfied with his role in the Tabernacle service, which God acknowledges with the gift of tithes.

Finally, God orders the Levites to give a portion of their tithes to Aaron and the priesthood. But this fourth order is no longer addressed to Aaron but to Moses, because it would be unseeming to have Aaron convey a revelation which enriches himself. (This nuance is pointed out by Ibn Ezra.)

Surprisingly, what follows next is the Torah's most mystical ritual, the law of the Red Heifer. The revelation comes to Moses and Aaron jointly; however, the preparation of the Red Heifer ashes – which will purify the impure but defile the pure – is entrusted to Elazar, Aaron's son, who in the course of the procedure is simply termed "the Priest." We have here a prefiguration of Aaron's demise, which comes shortly after Miriam's death, which is recorded in the very first verse after the Red Heifer chapter. This chapter obviously appears at a significant juncture, especially because its placement is not based on the sequence of events, since the Red Heifer ashes were already extant and used for purifying the Levites in the earlier 8th chapter. Further, the verses after the Red Heifer chapter find the Israelites in Kadesh, where they are at Edom's border and about to enter Canaan, after having spent the forty years in the desert. Thus, some 38 years elapsed between the events dated before the Red Heifer chapter and after. There is no statement in the text to acknowledge the time-lapse. Indeed, we recognized early on that the Book of Numbers is not organized primarily by chronology, but by grouped attitudes and perspectives. It seems that the mystical Red Heifer chapter serves as the transition for the events separated by 38 years, in the same way that Moses' parenthetical speech separated the string of "good" happenings from the "bad." Thus, the Red Heifer text includes forward-looking elements such as the upcoming priesthood of son Elazar, and also retrospective elements such as the fourth repeat that converts are equal under the law.

It is in their fortieth year in the wilderness that the people again rail against Moses and Aaron, saying, "We wish we had died with our brethren before the Lord, and why did you bring the Lord's nation into this desert to die, we and our flocks? Why did you take us from Egypt to lead us to this terrible place, without plants, figs, grapes, pomegranates, and with no water to drink!" (20:3). The uproarious tone of this complaint is just as offensive as that of the earlier riots, which brought on Divine threats of destruction, but here God calmly tells Moses: "Take the staff, you and Aaron your brother, speak to the rock before them and draw water for them from the rock, and let them and their animals drink." That the animals are being provided with water alongside the people – the animals being mentioned three times – indicates God's acceptance of their complaint, since His response extends to providing drink even for the animals. But Moses and Aaron respond to the crowds with this speech: "Listen up, you rebels, is it from this rock that you all expect us to tap water for you?" This rhetorical question is laced with bitter sarcasm, and withholds that God wishes to please the people and gladly provide the needed water. Then, instead of speaking to the rock, Moses angrily hits the rock twice, signifying to the crowd that it is they who deserve to be beaten repeatedly. Here we have a reverse of the usual respective responses by God and by Moses. Thirty-eight years earlier we had Divine threats and prayers by Moses. Imagining forty years of complaining, we can understand how the man Moses would lose patience, and indeed Moses had pleaded early on, telling God that he could no longer bear the whole nation's demands (11:11). Still, because they misrepresented God's sacred kindness here, Moses and Aaron were told they had lost the right to lead and that they would die on this side of Jordan, before going to the Promised Land.

Nonetheless, the ever faithful Moses goes on doing whatever he can to advance the people's arrival to the Holy Land, and he begins to represent the people on the international scene. He contacts the King of Edom with a friendly tone, reminding of Edom's relations with Israel going back to the patriarchal period when Jacob and Esau the Edomite parted ways. Moses asks permission to use Edom for a shortcut to Canaan. The Edomites say no and mobilize their army. Israel departs, going the long way around, until it becomes time for the death of Aaron, by the word of God. The ever-loyal Moses arranges for the ceremonious transfer of Aaron's priesthood to son Elazar. Moving ever closer to Canaan, Israel encounters an attack by the Canaanites of Arad. Israel prays directly to God for help and is victorious.

But the people are weary and go on complaining to Moses, "Why did you take us out of Egypt to die in this desert? There is no food and no water and we are sick of this cruddy meal." God punishes them with swarms of poisonous snakes. But the people quickly repent and apologize to Moses, so that God orders Moses to erect a copper replica of a serpent, and to have anyone bitten by a snake look at the replica and be healed.

There is in this latest incident some optimism, even playfulness. The "sh" or "s" sounds which are heard in the Hebrew for snake, *nachash*, occur some fifteen times in three of these verses to mimic the snake's hiss. There is a relaxed tone of accommodation and then snatches of song and poetry that project Israel onto an international setting. With this new confidence, Israel turns to the serious business of conquest. Under Moses' able leadership, the Israelites defeat and replace the two major Transjordanian powers, the Amorites under Sichon and those under Og.

These victories advance Israel to the edge of the Jordan River, on the plains of Moab facing Jericho. Taking note of Israel's advances and filled with dread was Balak King of Moab. He hires the famed soothsayer Balaam to come from Midian to curse Israel, adding, "For I know that anyone you bless is blessed and anyone you curse is cursed." What follows is a demonstration of how mindful God is of Israel's welfare. Balaam dreams of God advising him to stay home, not to curse Israel. Nonetheless Balaam starts out, riding on this donkey. The donkey is shown an angel thrusting a sword into their path. The donkey weaves about, and Balaam whips his donkey repeatedly. Then God has the donkey speak in its own defense, and it wins the argument when God finally allows Balaam to see the sword-drawn angel. Of course the joke is on Balaam, hired because he has the power to destroy with his tongue but losing a debate against an animal, and looking especially foolish because he had told the donkey, "If I had a sword in hand I would slay you." So as the prior chapters featured song, poetry, and mimicry, now the narrative has moved to irony in order to mock Israel's enemies. God's defense of His Chosen People extended to staging a scene with angels and donkeys, so as to turn Israel's enemies into laughing stocks.

It is worth noting that the Divine responses in the Book of Numbers often come with a surprise that may leave the reader breathless. Here we are astonished by a talking donkey; then Balaam mouths a blessing when he meant a curse; Israel's punishment comes via a swarm of snakes; the antidote is simply to look at a copper snake; a man orders a rock to produce water; the Red Heifer purifies the foul but contaminates the pure; Aaron's staff sprouts ripe almonds; Korach is punished when the earth swallows him; Israel is sentenced to forty years in the wilderness for forty days of spying; Miriam is punished with leprosy; Moses' spirit flashes onto 70 prophets; God provides meat by flying in quail; a make-up Passover is legislated on request; an unfaithful wife is cleared or condemned by her drinking a potion with God's name. Because the Book of Numbers is about how God wishes to relate to Israel, the Divine character is expressed in the limitless bounds of its transcendental nature, which leaves the human reader in a daze.

Meanwhile, Balaam continues on to Moab, expecting to collect a fat fee for a curse of Israel. Balak, his host, prepares a mountain-top setting for Balaam's oracle. But God interferes with Balaam's speech, so that he pronounces two beautiful poems of praise for Israel. Finally, the much touted power of Balaam's tongue is realized with his now famous, "How goodly are your tents, O Jacob, and your neighborhoods, O Israel," concluding with, "May those who bless you be blessed, and those who curse you be cursed." This last line enraged Balak because of the implied curse upon himself.

But the men of Israel, unaware of God's stunning activities on their behalf, began to consort with the Moabite young ladies, who then invited them to join in Moabite pagan worship. When Moses begins the legal proceedings against the guilty men, Zimri, a prince of Reuben, takes a voluptuous Midianite princess and, within sight of Moses and the elders, secludes himself with her. Zimri's motive was to save his men from prosecution for dallying with Midianite or Moabite women, arguing that Moses himself had married a Midianite, his wife Tzipora. At this brazen affront Moses broke down in tears. Saving the day came an agile Pinchas, son of Elazar, who understood that Zimri's act was an attack on Israel's honor. Grabbing a spear, he broke into the couple's bedroom and stabbed them to death. The Divine response: "Pinchas ben Elazar ben Aaron the Priest, has stilled my anger against the Children of Israel, by acting zealously on My behalf, so that I would not destroy the Children of Israel with a vengeance. Therefore proclaim, I extend to him My covenant for peace ..." (25:10). Pinchas' apt violent move won for him a God-given peace prize. Pinchas embodies the new-generation leadership, in step with the news of Moses' imminent demise, and the recent demonstration of how Moses can use the help of young blood in Israel's management. And when God orders Moses to start a war of retaliation against Midian, it is Pinchas who Moses sends into battle to support the army.

This war of retaliation was against Midian, but not against Moab. Why not against Moab as well? It seems that Moab could be forgiven, because after all, Israel was camped at its border, on the Plains of Moab, which however Moab had lost to the Amorites in a previous war. But the Midianites came from another land to join the fray, invited because they had close political relations with Moab (22:4). And while the Moabite girls may have come out to the Israelite men with excessive friendship, still it may have been the men who instigated the dalliance. But the intrusion of a Midianite princess in the fray, certainly pointed to a government authorized attack on Israel's integrity, intended to create havoc. Beyond this justification, the text has shown how Balaam, coming from Midian, refused to bend to God's wishes that he not curse Israel, and how God had to deal with his perdition in three full chapters, 22, 23, and 24. So the retaliation against Midian was Israel's and God's.

From this point until the end of the book there are no "bad" events that mar Israel's relations with her God. In ways, these final chapters of Numbers mirror the book's idyllic beginning. Chapter 26 has God ordering, "Take a headcount of the entire nation of Israel, of those twenty years and older, by family, all those who are of draft age." It was with a headcount that the book began, some 38 years earlier. But this new census has a new method and a new purpose.

This census adds the names of family groups within each tribe. For example: "Reuben, Israel's firstborn: The sons of Reuben, Enoch now the Enochite family; for Palu the Paluite family; for Chetzron the Chetzronite family; for Carmi the Carmite family. These are Reuben's families, numbering 43,730 persons." The reason for the added family names becomes clear after some 50 verses of the census. These named families are to be the primary inheritors of estates in Canaan: "The Lord told Moses, 'It is to these that you should apportion the land for inheritance, counting up those named. For the populous increase the inheritance and for the few reduce the inheritance, giving each its inheritance based on its number. However, the land is to be divided by lot among the named patriarchal tribes; their inheritance will be apportioned by lot, whether many or few'" (26:52).

The expected entrance into Canaan is the overarching theme of all that follows in Numbers from this point on. The Levites are counted separately, as was done in chapter one, but the reason given here for the separate tally is in line with the ongoing theme: The tribe of Levi will not get a portion in the land (26:62).

Then five sisters, the daughters of one Tzelafchad, approach Moses and the leaders with a claim seeking a part of the Holy Land, whereas only men were listed to represent the families. Their father had been eligible for a portion but had died in the desert leaving no male offspring. The sisters wanted his assigned portion and wanted to commemorate their father in this way. Moses placed their request before God.

This petition by five virtuous women advances the ongoing theme about the Holy Land. This petition also mirrors the request at the beginning of Numbers (9:6) by the virtuous men who refused to be left out of the Passover sacrifice. In each case Moses turns to God and in each case God's answer satisfies the petitioner. Here Moses is told to grant the inheritance to the five praiseworthy sisters – whose names are inscribed in the Torah three times – using a heretofore unknown ruling about how a daughter may inherit a father who has no son.

Moses had been faithfully preparing the nation to take possession of Canaan, when God repeats that he will not go there: "Climb this bordering mountain and gaze upon the land which I have given the Children of Israel. Behold it, then pass away, as your brother Aaron, too, died" (27:12).

Ever the dutiful leader, Moses answers, "Let the Lord, overlord of the spirit of men, appoint someone over the nation who can lead them and gather them ... so that the Lord's people will not be shepherdless" (27:16). God names Joshua, and Moses places his hands over him, appointing him the next leader for all to see.

What follows is a 70-verse-long section detailing the sacrifices required for every day and every holiday in the year, with a total of over 300 animal sacrifices. The language is drawn-out, preferring repeats over brevity, and mirroring the drawn-out language at Numbers' beginning which detailed in over 70 verses the identical contributions of the twelve princes (7:12). We must wonder how this section fits into the ongoing theme. The answer may rest with the section's introduction: "The Lord spoke to Moses as follows: 'Command the Children of Israel telling them, make sure to remember to sacrifice to Me my sacrificial bread at the right time, my fire offering and my aromatic incense. Say to them, this is the fire offering which you are to offer the Lord . . .'" (28:1).

The first verse here is shocking both in its demanding tone and in its figurative language, which would convey that Divinity requires animal sacrifices the way humans need bread. The Book of Leviticus, the primary full-length treatment of the sacrificial code, assiduously avoids both of these impressions, as our study of Leviticus has shown. But this Numbers context is controlled by the news that Moses is about to die, and thus will no longer be available for God to reveal the secrets of existence. It is here, to the still living Moses, that God hurries to reveal the deeply mysterious necessity of having man worship at God's altar. But so that the average listener not be misled, the next verse has God instructing Moses, "Say to them [simply], this is the fire offering which you are to offer the Lord."

How the next section, chapter 30, fits into the overarching theme needs study as well. Here we have Moses laying down the laws of vows, the honoring of one's pledge, a father's control over a daughter's oath, and when a husband may interfere with a wife's promise, concluding with, "If the husband annuls them after his first hearing about them, he is to bear her sin. These are the rules which the Lord commanded Moses regarding the relationship between husband and wife, and between father and daughter while she is a girl in her father's home" (30:16).

This section may be here because of what follows in God's next statement to Moses: "Enact Israel's revenge against the Midianites, and thereafter you are to pass away" (31:2). The ever-obedient Moses organizes the nation for war, the Israelites are victorious, and the army returns from Midian loaded with spoils and captives. Moses explodes in anger on seeing the multitude of female captives: "Are these not the ones who caused the Children of Israel to sin against the Lord at Peor, because of Balaam, and resulting in the plague which befell the Chosen People? Now kill every male child and kill every woman who has had relations with a man. But every girl who did not have relations with a man, keep alive for yourselves" (31:15).

The text then informs that there were 32,000 underage girls. Based on this figure the population of marriageable female captives must have been over 100,000. What happened to them? We are not told that Moses' angry order was carried out, in what would have been a sickening slaughter. For the soldiers who brought these women from Midian – perhaps keeping order and providing food and water – it would have been a tough command to obey. If these men were able to accomplish such a horrendous task, the text would characteristically have noted their phenomenal obedience, but nothing is mentioned. Maybe the captive women found that they were unwanted and were no longer restrained, and they made their way back to Midian with their male children. If this is what happened, it explains how Midian resurfaced as an international power and even defeated Israel two hundred years later, as reported in the Book of Judges, chapter 6.

Moses' angry and belated order should be understood alongside his prior confrontation with Zimri and the Midianite princess, when Moses broke down and cried. A personal factor, the fact that a young Moses had found haven in Midian while escaping Pharaoh's wrath and had married into a leading Midianite family, introduced a self-conscious element into his present dealings with Midian, resulting in some indecisiveness. And Moses' familial connection with Midian is recalled earlier in Numbers, "Said Moses to Chovav ben Reuel the Midianite, his father-in-law, 'We are off to the land the Lord said He would give us. Come with us ...'" (10:28).

But so that Moses' outburst to kill the captive women not be misunderstood as a general insensitivity to women, the laws about the wives and daughters appear first, featuring a conclusion which bases the relationships between men and women, between fathers and daughters, and between husbands and wives on a fair mutual understanding. Accordingly, this section on the laws of oaths begins on Moses' own initiative, without the expected Divine cue (30:2), so that the reader will have the two speeches about womanhood side by side.

Further, the army commanders are viewed as innocent and praiseworthy before God and Moses when they donate the captured gold to the Tabernacle: "Moses and Elazar the Priest accepted the gold from the generals and captains, placing it in the Tabernacle as a memento from the Children of Israel before the Lord" (31:54). These donations by the commanders mirror the donations of wagons by the princes of Israel in early Numbers, and are seen as equally praiseworthy. Along the same lines, the drawn-out mathematical calculations of the number of animals divided between the soldiers and the citizenry are also reminiscent of Numbers' beginning.

A multitude of grazing animals features again in the next event, and it also returns us to the theme of the advance to Canaan. "The men of Reuben and Gad came and said … 'This [Amorite] land which the Lord defeated for the Children of Israel is grazing land and we, your servants, have flocks. Kindly give this land to us for our inheritance; do not cross us over the Jordan.' Said Moses to the men of Gad and Reuben, 'Shall your brethren go to war while you dwell here?'" (32:2). But Moses goes on to negotiate an agreement that if Reuben and Gad spearhead the nationwide attack on Canaan they would have Transjordan for their promised land. Of course, Moses would not be there to enforce the agreement, but ever the trusted leader, he worked for the good of Israel into the future. And here, contrary to Moses' consulting God as he did with the petition of Tzelafchad's daughters, Moses decides on his own competence. God's agreement with Moses' decision comes only indirectly, when at the end of the book God names just nine princes for apportioning Canaan, omitting princes for Reuben and Gad as unnecessary (34:16). Also on his own, Moses encourages the warriors of Menashe to conquer additional cities in Transjordan, and he bequeaths these cities to the tribe of Menashe.

A full retrospect of Moses' leadership is then enshrined in the Torah, starting from the deliverance from Egypt to the present:

"Moses wrote down the stops in their travels as the Lord had ordered" (33:2). The text then lists the 42 travel stops of Israel's 40
years of wandering in the wilderness. It seems that this was a distinct document that God ordered Moses to inscribe a copy of, or
version of, in the Torah as an appreciation of Moses' leadership.
The few comments added to the bare listing are instructive: Mention is made of where the Israelites had or did not have water, or
where they suffered an enemy attack, but the Ten Commandments
at Sinai and the wondrous parting of the Red Sea are glanced
over, mentioning instead instances where Moses' leadership came
into play. And the only lengthy excursus in the list tells of brother
Aaron's death, using some 30 words, while Aaron's own leading
role was being recognized with appreciation as well (33:1).

Alternatively, if this listing of Israel's travels is not seen as an
initial separate document, then God telling Moses to write the
travels into the Torah is meant to reflect on how all the Five Books
of Moses were composed by God's order to Moses. But a full treatment of how the Torah came into being is reserved for the final
chapters of Deuteronomy (31:24).

After this 49-verse listing for acknowledging Moses' years at
the helm, only God's own initiatives and commandments appear
through the end of Numbers, with Moses merely following God's
orders. God speaks now with powerful directness and with thun-
derous warnings against disobedience: "Tell the Children of Israel,
'You are going over the Jordan to the land of Canaan and you are
to drive off its inhabitants ... But if you do not expel the inhabitants of the land, then those you leave behind shall become like
cinders in your eyes and thorns in your sides. They shall terrorize
you in your homeland, so that what I had expected be done to
them I shall do to you'" (33:50).

After this dire warning, God turns to geography, identifying the
territory which constitutes the Promised Land, and announcing
the names of the tribes' princes who will apportion the land, under
Elazar and Joshua's oversight.

The Levites, so prominent at the book's beginning, are now recognized once more and are granted 48 cities, to be selected from
within the estates of the landed tribes. Six of these Levite cities will
serve as cities of refuge where an unintentional killer can find safe

haven: "These cities are to be a refuge from an avenger, so that the killer not perish before being judged by the people" (35:12).

The issue of murder and places of refuge was mentioned in three short verses in Exodus 21:12, but here we have the substantive law, as Israel prepares for real life in its land. We have 25 full verses on murder and manslaughter formulating the justice required for settlement: "So that you do not defile the land wherein you dwell, because spilled blood befouls the land, and the land will not be cleansed of its spilled blood except by the spiller's blood. Therefore do not pollute your homeland because I the Lord dwell there, dwelling among the Children of Israel" (35:33). With regard to manslaughter and unintentional homicide, "Let the community rescue the killer from the blood avenger's hands and let the community place him in the refuge city to which he ran, to remain there until the death of the high priest, who was anointed with the holy oil" (35:25).

The high priest is mentioned here four times but no reason is given for his death to release the killer. Exodus 21:12 reads, "Anyone who beats a man to death shall die. But if he did not stalk him and it was as if by an act of God, then I shall give you a place for escape." The term "act of God" reminds us that human beings are not fully in control of their surroundings, nor even of their own existence, for all mortals die eventually. This truth applies even to the purest man, such as the high priest, "who was anointed with the holy oil." His death asserts that all men die eventually, and renders the victim's death less tragic because no one lives forever. Further, "After the death of the high priest, let the killer return to the land of his own heritage" (35:28). This verse brings to mind that the killer had been exiled to a Levite city – all the cities of refuge were Levite cities – so that the high priest, as prince of Levi, was in effect an honorary landlord of the exiled killer, who with the high priest's demise returns to his own heritage.

The book ends on a happier note, which mirrors the "good" times at the book's beginning. The men of Menashe are concerned that they may lose territory in the Holy Land if the daughters of Tzelafchad – now being inheritors within Menashe – marry husbands from other tribes. The men's concern reflects a love for the Holy Land and their wanting to keep as much of the blessed soil as possible. On the other hand, it was a group from Menashe that had asked Moses to let them have Transjordan, which could be taken as an insult to the Holy Land. But here we have members of the same Menashe tribe expressing how they cherish the Holy Land and want to keep their fair share of it. God again satisfies His petitioners, and instructs the Tzelafchad girls to marry within their tribe – it being no problem for these virtuous, patriotic ladies to obey God and make peace in the family. Each of them marries a cousin and expectedly would live happily ever after.

That the book ends with a discussion of marriage may contribute to closure for the first four books of the Torah, as a group. The first four books, Genesis, Exodus, Leviticus and Numbers, have a common narrative genre, whereas the final of the Five Books of Moses, Deuteronomy, introduces itself as a copy of the speeches of Moses. Genesis' beginning gives prominence to marriage by having the first quoted human voice talk marriage. As Adam approached Eve, "The man said, 'This time we have bone of my bones and flesh of my flesh; she will be called "woman" because she comes from man.'" The very next verse is the first that addresses the reader directly and reflects on the culture of marriage in our own day: "Therefore does a man leave his father and his mother in order to bond with his wife, so that they become a single body" (Genesis 2:24). Thus, the conclusion of Numbers comes full circle, dwelling on God's matchmaking activity to close the four-book group, as an ongoing extension of His creation of marriage when the world began.

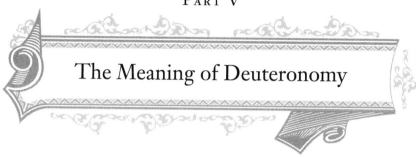

PART V

The Meaning of Deuteronomy

"THESE ARE THE WORDS which Moses spoke to all the Children of Israel in Transjordan ... It was in the fortieth year, on the first day of the eleventh month, that Moses conveyed to the Children of Israel all that the Lord commanded them...."

Deuteronomy introduces itself as the text of Moses' speeches, orations aimed at "clarifying this Torah." "This Torah" may refer to the Book of Deuteronomy, which follows, or to the first four books of the Torah, or to both. If the first books of the Torah express the Divine's perspective on the human experiment, then Deuteronomy promises a human view of the relationship with the Divine. Indeed, Moses' first quoted word is "the Lord": "The Lord spoke to us at Horeb saying, 'Enough now of your stay at this mountain. Depart for the Amorite mountain and environs, the valleys, the heights, the low lands, the Negev, the sea shore, the land of Canaan, the Lebanon, as far as the great Euphrates River. Look, I've given you this land, come take the land....'"

The Horeb mountain refers of course to Mount Sinai and to the giving of the Ten Commandments there, amid the supreme Divine revelation. This opening quote has God play down the glories of Sinai in favor of the bounties of the Holy Land. Accordingly, the aspiration for Israel's settlement in the Holy Land will remain the central theme and thrust of this book.

The term "Horeb" continues to appear – some half-dozen times

– instead of "Sinai," in Moses' orations. That he prefers the name Horeb may relate to the fact that Moses' first contact with the Mount of God, when he pastured the family sheep there, uses the term Horeb, in Exodus 3. Verse 2 of the book's introduction also uses "Horeb," bending to Moses' usage. In verse 4, the introduction also anticipates Moses' repeated reference to the victory over Og and Sichon the Amorites, mentioned whenever Moses wishes to reassure Israel that she can similarly vanquish the Canaanites, whom he occasionally calls the Amorites. Further, the introduction credits Moses himself with the victory over the Amorites, while in the Numbers 21 account, Israel as a whole is credited with the victory. But here Moses will soon deal with his own persona, his relationship with the nation, and the quality of his leadership: "I told you even then that I could not lead you by myself.... I could not by myself bear up under your troubles, challenges, and disputes ... So I took your tribal leaders – wise and recognized men – and placed them over you ..." (verse 9). Aware that he would not be there to lead them into Canaan, that he would die during the year, Moses tells the people that they have other competent leadership, so that Moses' demise not cause them to lose heart when going to war. This is why Moses here brings up the appointment of the tribal leaders, whereas the original account in Exodus 18 conveys a different perspective.

Next, Moses reminds the people of what happened at the very start of their forty years in the desert, when Israel sent spies to scout out the Holy Land, and how the negative report of the spies disheartened the masses and filled them with fear. Here too, Moses' account differs from the omniscient narrator account in Numbers 13. For here Moses sets out to rebuke the people for having lost their faith in God, and to warn them not to repeat such sinning if they expect to conquer Canaan. Then, to make his rebuke more palatable, Moses adds: "The Lord was angry with me as well, because of you, and He said to me: 'You too shall not reach there'" (verse 37).

In chapter 2 Moses turns to the international scene in his ongoing effort to embolden Israel for the conquest of the Holy Land. So that Israel would not consider their upcoming attack as an act of lawless violence, Moses forbids them to threaten nearby Edom,

Moab, or Ammon, because God has bequeathed these territories to these peoples. Each had conquered an original occupant, mighty giants such as the Emim, the Horites, the Zamzumim, and the Avim who themselves were defeated by the Kaftorim islanders. Drawing the parallel to what God will have Israel do to the Canaanites, verse 12 has, "... just as Israel will have done for her inherited land, which the Lord has given them," framed so as to trigger their imagination with an accomplished fact.

As already foreshadowed in the book's introduction, God did order Moses to attack the Transjordanian Amorites: "See, I am presenting you with the conquest of Sichon, King of Cheshbon the Amorite and his land; begin the attack, incite warfare. Today I begin to spread the fear and fright of you over all the nations under the sky, who will tremble at the mention of your name" (2:24).

What follows is a drawn-out telling of the campaign against Sichon and Og, taking 35 leisurely verses, with specifics that are omitted in the earlier Numbers 21 account. Here Moses reports the victory in its international geographic setting: "We conquered Mount Hermon; the Sidonites call the Hermon Siryon, while the Amorites term it the Senir – and all the cities of the plains, all Gilead, all the Bashan as far as Salcha and Edrei, these being the habitations of the Og Kingdom in the Bashan. For only Og King of Bashan survived among the remaining Giants; behold, his cot, a cot made of iron, is still there in Rabbah of Ammon, it being nine cubits long and four standard cubits wide" (3:8). Moses is encouraging Israel to see itself acting in line with recognized realities.

Then Moses tells them, "I gave to the tribe of Reuben from Aroer, which is in the valley of Arnon, to half of Mount Gilead and its cities. The rest of Gilead and all the Og Kingdom I gave to half the tribe of Menashe ..." (3:12). While in the Numbers 32 account, the tribes of Reuben, Gad, and Menashe wrested these territories from a reluctant Moses, who argued against their request for Amorite land, here Moses turns the granting of their request into a gracious gift, so that the land grant will reflect positively on Israel's receiving its inheritance in Canaan.

"Then I pleaded with the Lord, saying: 'Lord God, You have begun to show Your servant, Your majesty and might – and which power in heaven or earth can replicate Your accomplished triumphs – please let me pass over to witness the good land which is beyond the Jordan …' But the Lord answered: 'Enough, don't talk to Me about this anymore …'" (3:23). Here again, Moses is dwelling on a conversation omitted in Numbers 27, where Moses accepts at once God's punishment of his having to die on this side of Jordan. But here Moses seeks to inspire the people with the glory of Holy Land, which he longs to enter, so that they will consider themselves fortunate with their prospects.

From chapter 4, Moses begins to expound the Torah's laws, already mentioned in the book's introduction: "Now Israel, hear the precepts and laws which I am teaching you, so that you live to reach and inherit the land which the Lord, God of your fathers, grants you." Thus, even when presenting the legislation, Moses allies it to the Holy Land setting. Even when referring to his prior lawgiving, and even including the spectacular giving of the Ten Commandments, Moses portrays the laws as intended for life in the Holy Land: "Look, I have taught you the precepts and laws which the Lord my God commanded me, in order for you to enact them in the heartland which you come to inherit" (4:6). The appeal to international public opinion surfaces again here: "Observe and enact them because they reflect your wisdom and sagacity in the eyes of the nations, who will notice all these laws and declare how wise and sagacious this great nation is" (4:6).

After a blunt warning not to desecrate their covenant with God, Moses formulates the theme of Exile and Redemption – or sinning and repentance – which will feature some half-dozen times in Deuteronomy, and which is rendered in verse in the so-called Song of Moses, chapter 32. "When you have children, grandchildren, and become old-timers in the land, if you sin by making idols of whatever shape, doing evil in the eyes of the Lord your God and upsetting Him, I warn you before heaven and earth that you will soon be exiled from the land which you cross the Jordan to inherit … But when you seek after the Lord from there, you will reach Him if you pursue Him with your whole heart and soul …" (4:25).

Suddenly, Moses' ongoing speeches are interrupted by narration: "Moses then designated three cities on the eastern side of the Jordan, where a homicide – one who unintentionally kills someone against whom he never had a grudge – may run to and live there ..." (4:41). This interruption is justified by the return of the book's introduction, which had briefly mentioned God's teachings, and which now reintroduces the Torah's laws as being the subject of Moses' next oration: "These are the testaments, the precepts, and the laws which Moses presented to the Children of Israel when they left Egypt, when they were in Transjordan ..." (4:45).

This singling out of Moses setting up the cities of refuge illustrates that Moses himself took the initiative to obey the laws he preaches, even in Transjordan, in anticipation of settlement in the real Holy Land. Further, the mention of the cities of refuge creates a literary bridge between the theme of the first oration – the surge toward Holy Land settlement – and the theme of the upcoming oration – obedience to the laws. Indeed, the final verse of the first oration echoes this switch: "Keep His precepts and commandments which I command you this day, so that you and your children after you will succeed, and so that you shall forever live on the land which the Lord your God gives you" (4:40).

Moses begins his teaching by citing the Ten Commandments. This is Moses' second mention of the Ten Commandments in Deuteronomy, but this time he pronounces the whole text, and then uses it as a springboard for all the laws.

However, Moses' rendition of the Ten Commandments here is not word-for-word identical with the Exodus 20 text. There is no variation at all in Moses' rendition of the first two Commandments, where God is presenting in the grammatical first person "I am the Lord your God ..." But in the Sabbath command, Moses adds his own admonition, "... as the Lord your God commanded you." Then verse 15 has, "So remember that you were a slave in Egypt ... Therefore did the Lord your God command you to observe the Sabbath day," whereas the Exodus text has "... because the Lord created heaven and earth in six days; and reposed on the seventh day." Then in the command against coveting, Exodus has not coveting a neighbor's house as the caption, while Moses places not coveting a neighbor's wife as the caption, then lists the house with the remaining objects. It seems that Moses, as man, admonishes the other men to warn that coveting a wife is the most dangerous sin, while God's words in Exodus apply to men and women more evenly, so that the caption cites coveting the house.

Next, Moses offers an explanation for his assuming the role of purveyor of the Divine law. He reminds the populace that upon hearing the voice of God, they were so affrighted that they pleaded with Moses, "You go and listen to all that the Lord our God propounds, then you tell us all that the Lord our God tells you, and we shall listen and obey" (5:24). Moses further reminds them that God had concurred, telling him, "So you stand here with Me and I shall convey to you all the commandments, precepts, and laws which you are to teach them, to enact in the land which I am giving them as a heritage" (5:28).

While this oration is about the laws, the earlier theme of Holy Land settlement remains prominent, and reappears again as a dangling modifier in 6:3, ". . . a land flowing with milk and honey."

Moses teaches, "Hear O Israel, the Lord our God, the Lord is one," and goes on to obligate Israel in the love of God, in cherishing his directives, and in doing what is right – that when God delivers Canaan to them, they not adopt the pagan divinities there, but remember the Lord. That when their children will ask about the religious traditions, they explain their allegiance to God through the nation's history – taught as a lesson meant also for Moses' immediate audience. That when they become settled in the land, they not integrate with the pagan peoples, "Do not intermarry with them. Give not your daughters to their sons and take not their daughters for your sons. Thereby would your sons be diverted to worship other divinities, so that the anger of the Lord burn against you to quickly destroy you" (7:3).

At this point, Moses portrays the blessedness which will come from their allegiance to God's law: "As reward for your observing and upholding these laws, the Lord your God will uphold the covenant and kindness which He promised your forefathers. He shall love you, bless you, and multiply you . . ." (7:12).

Having rendered the love which Israel owes God reciprocal – stating that God loves Israel as well – Moses proceeds with full confidence in addressing the nation. Never before was Israel's desert experience pictured in terms of such harsh reality: "Remember the forty-year-long desert trek which the Lord your God assigned you, in order to harden you, to test you, to determine just what is in your heart, whether or not you will keep His commandments

... because the Lord your God disciplines you the way a father disciplines his son" (8:2). Never before was the Canaanite enemy acknowledged as being so powerful: "Hear O Israel, today you traverse the Jordan to overtake nations greater and mightier than you, with large cities with fortifications reaching the sky. A great people, hulking giants such as you've heard how none can oppose such giants" (9:1).

But then Moses warns them against self-righteousness and triumphalism: "When the Lord your God defeats them for you, do not say to yourselves, 'It is my righteousness which led the Lord to bequeath this land to me, plus the wickedness of these nations.' No, it is not your righteousness or honesty which has you conquer their land; rather it is the wickedness of those nations" (9:4).

This rebuke triggers a 28-verse history of Israel's shortcomings: "... you are a stiff-necked people. Recall how you provoked the Lord your God in the desert ... reaching here you were repeatedly rebellious before the Lord" (9:6). Moses turns for a third time to the giving of the Ten Commandments, but in this instance it is to the adjacent sin of the Golden Calf, which turned the Sinai revelation into a tragedy. The present version follows the Exodus 32 account closely, except for the addition about Aaron: "And against Aaron too did the Lord wax angry to destroy him, and I prayed for Aaron at that time" (9:20).

Also unknown in the Exodus account is the incident about the wooden ark which Moses made to house the replacement Tablets of the Law: "I made an ark of acacia wood; I hewed two stone tablets like the originals ... God wrote on the tablets the replicated text of the Ten Commandments ... I descended the mountain and put the tablets in the ark I had made, where they remained, as the Lord ordered me" (10:3). In effect, this account brushes aside the creation of a Tabernacle, which is so prominent in Exodus 25–40, and in which the tablets were ultimately housed. Further, the Tabernacle is not mentioned at all by Moses in any of his Deuteronomy orations. These facts are the reason for the sudden return of the narration here, running from chapter 10, verse 6 through verse 9. Not only is Aaron mentioned again, but his son Elazar who inherited the priesthood is named, and beyond the priesthood, mention is made of Moses' entire tribe, the Levites, who were selected "to bear the Ark of the Lord's Covenant, to stand before the Lord in service, and to bless in His name, unto this very day." All this relates to Moses personally. Consequently, the narration is made to interrupt Moses' speech, lest he sound self-serving or proud, and to deal with these points impersonally. What is more, this avoids having Moses dwell upon or even mention the Tabernacle's Ark of the Covenant. For shortly, Moses will be introducing a competing ideal, one which is central to the overarching thrust of his orations, namely, a new requirement for the national life in the Holy Land, that there be a single, sacred space for worship: "Only at that place which the Lord your God will choose from within all your tribes to rest His aura – there shall you go to seek His presence. There shall you bring your offerings ... there to dine before the Lord your God and rejoice" (12:5).

The phrase, "the place which God will choose," is repeated almost two dozen times, but is never before found in Scripture. It is a formulaic, set phrase that conceals as much as it reveals – and which only future history will reveal as referring to a sanctuary in Jerusalem, as present-day readers realize.

It seems that the neglect of the wilderness Tabernacle in Moses' speeches is meant to emphasize the directives on settlement in the Promised Land. Thus, we have repeated mention of this requirement for sacred service somewhere in the Holy Land, in a mystical location known only to God.

Toward preparing to legislate this striking new directive, Moses introduces other items which involve the geography of the Holy Land: "The land which you are coming to inherit is not like the land of Egypt which you left behind, where one plants his seeds and must walk about to water them, like a vegetable garden. But the land that you are entering to inherit is a land of hills and valleys, where you will imbibe the waters of heavenly rain. It is a land which the Lord your God checks steadily ... tending to it from year's start to finish" (11:10).

The geography concerning Mount Gerizim and Mount Ebal also precedes mention of the place that God will choose. Moses dwells on the terrain: "When the Lord your God brings you to the land you are coming to inherit, you are to place the Benediction on Mount Gerizim and the Malediction on Mount Ebal – are they not on the sunset side of the Jordan in the land of the Canaanites who occupy the plains facing Gilgal, near Elon Moreh" (11:29). But the text for the Benediction and Malediction, plus the procedures for a nationwide ceremony, is not presented until late in the book, in chapter 27, closer to the expected event.

There being a sacred space which God will choose has many ramifications, and the text sets out to deal with them: "When the Lord your God widens your boundaries ... so that the place which the Lord your God selects to place His aura there becomes far from you, you may properly slaughter of your cattle and sheep – which the Lord gives you – and eat to your heart's content within your cities. Eat them the way you would eat deer or gazelle, with impure and pure persons together ... However, your sacrifices and pledges must you transport and come to the place which God will select" (12:20).

Next are presented three cases of attempts to missionize for the pagan religions of the land. The first, an attempt by a wonder-working prophet, the second by a relative or dear friend, and the third by lawless individuals who succeed in turning their townspeople into idolaters. In the third instance, the town is sentenced to be burned and the inhabitants executed. The notion that such a dreadful scene could occur in the Holy Land causes the pendulum to swing to an opposite direction, with Moses reassuring Israel, "You are the children of the Lord your God. Do not mutilate or gash yourselves for the dead, because you are a holy nation ..." (14:1). This praise is enlarged by restricting them to the purest food sources; they are too good to imbibe disgusting things. What follows is a reassertion of the Kosher food regulations as found in Leviticus' 11th chapter.

The next laws are arranged by the number of years involved, from 1 to 3 to 7: "Take a tithe of your field's grain every single year, so as to eat it before the Lord your God at the place which he will choose ..." (14:22). Then, "After three years, bring out your produce's tithe and put it at your gates. Then can come the Levite – who has no part in your land inheritance – and the stranger, and the orphan, and the widow, who are at your gates, to eat and be satisfied ..." (14:25).

Then, "After seven years declare a remission. The remission

means that no creditor shall bother his fellow or brother ..."
(15:1). Further, "Should you have a poverty-stricken person in
a city in your land, which the Lord your God gives you, do not
be stingy ... Open your hand to give him whatever he needs ..."
(15:7). Further, "If you are sold a Hebrew slave or maid, have him
work for six years but on the seventh year send him off free ...
and tip him with a gift of your sheep, grain, and wine – giving him
from the blessings of the Lord your God to you ..." (15:12).

Switching back from doing what is right by man, the text turns
again to the service of the Creator, and in each new case there is
the recognition of the mystical sacred space: "Every firstborn calf
or lamb, if male, shall you sanctify for the Lord ... Dine on it before the Lord your God, year by year, at the place which the Lord
shall choose ..." (15:19). What follows is a reordering of the three
festival holidays, already treated in Exodus, Leviticus, and Numbers, but never before was each festival celebration associated with
the holy place which God will yet sanctify. Again in a summary,
"Three times a year shall every man be presented before the Lord
your God at the place He will select, on the Festival of Passover,
the Festival of Weeks, and the Festival of Booths ..." (15:16).

Concluding the leisurely presentation of the yearly holidays, the
text turns to the everyday business of the marketplace: "Establish
judges and court officers throughout your settlements, which the
Lord your God grants your tribes, so they can judge the people
justly" (16:18). Indeed, the courts will also rule on sins against Divinity (17:1), but they importantly must rule on ideological questions that threaten to splinter the nation's unity, and in such decisions the theme of a sacred place is remembered: "If the correct
judgment eludes you ... fomenting disputes at your gates, then
rise you up to that place which the Lord your God will choose.
Come to the priests, Levites, and judges of the day, to ask and to
have them declare for you what is right ..." (17:8).

The idea of a normative life in their own country, is now extended to the area of political life: "When you arrive in the land
which the Lord your God gives you ... and you declare, 'Let me
appoint me a king, just like all the peoples around me.' Yes, appoint yourselves a king, but one approved by the Lord ... Then
when he is settled on his throne, let him write a manuscript copy

of this Torah, the scroll shown by the priests and Levites. Let him keep it to read it all the days of his life, so that he will learn to fear the Lord his God, to observe the entire Torah, and to enact these precepts" (17:14).

Here we have the first mention of the Torah being a written document, a scroll volume. Mentioned here in passing, the Torah scroll's creation is taken up directly later on, in Deuteronomy 31.

The priests and Levites having just been pictured as keepers of the authentic Torah – and earlier as being functionaries at the court of justice – are allotted their just due, here in chapter 18 through verse 8. Of course Moses himself is a Levite, so that a self-conscious tone enters, and the voice of Moses rebounds in a personal way: "The nations whom you are overtaking listen to soothsayer and magicians, but the Lord your God lets you dispense with such. The Lord your God will appoint a prophet from your midst just like me, for you to follow. For this is what you requested of the Lord your God at Horeb on the day of the great assembly, 'Let me not hear anymore the voice of the Lord my God, nor witness this burning conflagration, lest I perish.' So the Lord said to me, 'They have spoken well. I shall present them with a prophet from their midst just like you ...'" (18:14).

However, when we read the original exchange in Exodus 20:15, the upcoming prophet is Moses himself, not a subsequent replacement. Moses' account here comes with the awareness of his own demise, that Israel's existence beyond the Jordan must go on without him, but with some other prophet. Still, it is possible that Moses' version here combines the Exodus 20 exchange with the Exodus 23:20 revelation: "I will send before you a ministering angel to protect you enroute and to deliver you to the place which I have readied ... ," if the ministering angel includes an allusion to Moses' successor prophet.

Projecting ahead to when Israel is fully settled, Moses legislates the establishment of the cities of refuge: "Set aside three cities in your homeland, which the Lord your God bequeaths to you, where any homicide can flee. But to stay alive there, he must have killed the person unintentionally, a person whom he did not despise ... But if a man hates a fellow, preys on him, jumps upon him, and strikes him dead to run away to one of these cities, then the elders of his town shall extricate him from there and turn him over to the next of kin for execution. Do not look away, but cleanse Israel of such innocent spilled blood and you shall prosper" (19:2).

These laws of the refuge cities vis-à-vis the laws of cold-blooded murder were already presented at the end of the Book of Numbers, chapter 35 with 34 verses. Certainly these laws have a special relevance in Deuteronomy, as Israel prepares to enter the land and occupy the refuge cities. Indeed, the refuge cities were already mentioned in this book (4:41), where the narration interrupted Moses' orations. Murder and manslaughter were also briefly legislated in Exodus 21:12, bringing the Torah's total for such legislation to some 50 verses. It may be that such inordinate attention stems from the fratricide of Cain and Abel in early Genesis, where the first two men born of woman enact a murder, and explains why this primordial dread remains constant in human history.

Chapter 19, from verse 16 and on, deals with how a wicked person may attempt to use the courts to do his killing, "Should a vicious liar testify to condemn a person … Let the judges search diligently to discover that, behold the witness is a liar, he testified falsely against his neighbor. Consequently, do to him what he schemed to do to his neighbor, and erase this evil from your midst … Do not look away …" The phrase "Do not look away," is the same phrase used above to justify the execution of a cold-blooded murderer, and this is why the law of the false witness follows here.

Indeed, the courts are expected to dispense criminal justice however harsh, concluding with, "A soul for a soul, an eye for an eye, a tooth for a tooth, a hand for a hand, a foot for a foot." Then when the Torah turns next to the violence of war, there emerges an attitude of consideration, to prevent the harshness from being an acceptable attitude in general: "Let the officers say to the assembled, 'Any man who has built a new house but which he did not yet inaugurate, let him return home, lest he die in battle, then would another man inaugurate it.'" The same draft exemption is then applied to any man who planted a vineyard but did not yet harvest it, or any man who betrothed a wife but did not yet husband her. And finally, "Any man who is afraid or weak-hearted let him return home, so that he not inspire fear in his brethren's hearts, such as is in his heart" (20:5).

Staying with the wartime setting, "When you approach a city to do battle, call to it for a negotiated peace ... But if it chooses to fight ... smite all the soldiery with the sword. Then take the women, children, animals, and everything in the city for yourselves as booty ... However, from the cities of those nations which the Lord your God gives you as your inheritance, take no living captive. Rather, totally destroy those, the Hittite, the Amorite, the Canaanite, Perizite, Hivite, and Jebusite, as the Lord your God commands you, so that they not teach you all their abominations ..." (20:10).

Again, lest one take the final violent scene to indicate that wanton rage is acceptable in the heat of battle, the pendulum swings to the opposite extreme, to indicate that even in war one must think twice before destroying even trees: "When you lay siege to a city for many days to capture it, do not destroy its trees by chopping with your axes, because you will be eating from them – for is it the tree or the person you are attacking during this siege? Only a tree that you know is not a fruit tree may you chop down ..." (20:19).

At this, a reader may mistakenly conclude that the protection of the environment is as important as human life, but the pendulum again swings back to demonstrate the supreme value of a person: "When, in the land which the Lord your God bequeaths to you, a slain corpse is found on the ground and the killer is unknown ... Have the elders of the nearest city bring out a young calf which never worked and never pulled a plow. Have the elders of the city take the calf to a dry gulch that is barren and cannot be cultivated, there to behead the calf in the gulch ... Then the elders are to wash their hands over the beheaded calf and declare, 'Our hands did not spill this blood, we saw nothing ...'" (21:1).

Of course, the tragedy depicted here deals with the death of a citizen. But the text again switches back to the wartime setting for a demonstration of sensitivity even for enemy captives: "If among the captives, you come across a beautiful woman, whom you desire and would take for a wife ... let her live in your house to mourn her father and mother for a month, then you may husband her to take as your wife. But if then you do not want her, set her free – do not sell or work her, because you did wrong her" (21:10).

The consideration expressed here for this woman may mistakenly be interpreted as support for the feminine or for the prevailing rights of wives in domestic situations. The ruling that follows mitigates such a one-sided view: Thus, if a man's beloved wife wants him to name her son as the privileged firstborn, whereas in fact the son of another wife was born first, the true firstborn's rights prevail over the beloved wife's wishes. Then this ruling may create the false impression that the rights of children are always dominant, as some cultures maintain. So now the pendulum swings to presenting a child in a losing situation: "If a man has a delinquent, rebellious son who disobeys his father and mother, and they discipline him but he doesn't listen. So his father and mother may grab him . . . and say to the city elders, 'This our son is delinquent and rebellious, he does not listen to us, only drinks and stuffs himself.' Then let all the inhabitants of his town stone him to death, and rid yourselves of what is evil in your midst . . ." (21:18).

But even such a death sentence does not deprive a person of his claim to human dignity in death, as the next law demonstrates: "When a man is executed for his sin and you hang him, do not leave his corpse hanging overnight, but give him proper burial on the same day . . ." (21:22).

From this recognition of a human's body, the law moves to the preservation of personal property, and then to the sensitivity due domestic animals: "Do not look away when you spot a fellow's loaded donkey or ox collapsing along the road; rather join in setting it aright" (22:4).

This mingling of the human and animal spheres culminates in the bird-nest law: "If you come across a bird's nest . . . with the mother sitting on the chicks or eggs, do not take the mother on/ guarding the children. Free the mother and you may take the children . . ." (22:6).

The continual use here of the term "mother and children," points to the human parallel involving a mother and her children. The unique expression "a mother on/guarding the children" occurs in its appropriate human context in Genesis 31:12, "Save me from my brother Esau, for I am afraid of him, lest he attack me and kill mothers on/guarding the children." There Jacob was imagining the dreadful scene wherein frenzied mothers respond to marauders by trying mightily to protect their children, even thrusting their own bodies in the way of the sword, as otherwise timid women turn into lionesses in defense of their offspring. The bird-nest law wants a hunter to realize that it is the same maternal instinct that his mother has which is causing the mother bird to protect her brood at her own peril. The bird-nest law tells us not to take advantage of the maternal instinct, even in a bird, to harm the mother and to make a meal of her.

Through chapter 25, the text continues with some four dozen additional laws, covering the gamut of situations which may confront Israel once settled on its soil. These situations touch on the animal, the spiritual, the aesthetic, family, business, nature, kindness, the military, the sexual, the racial, the ritual, vengeance, tradition, national memory, labor, health and safety, honesty, agriculture, housing, criminal justice, and war. A close reading often explains how one topic flows from the prior one, at times based on language.

Chapter 23, verses 7through 15, orders cleanliness for the army camp when engaged in battling a foreign enemy. Then verse 16 orders, "Do not return a runaway slave to his master when he wants asylum from his master. Let him dwell in your midst, wherever he wishes in one of your cities. Do not oppress him." The prior military setting remains the setting for the asylum-seeking slave, who thus managed to reach the army camp or Hebrew mainland. This is followed by, "There is not to be a holy prostitute among the daughters of Israel, nor a male prostitute among the sons of Israel" (23:18). This prohibition follows the acceptance of the foreign runaway, who could influence the society negatively if his or her absorption makes for foreign influence. Thus the harlot is termed a holy prostitute, which was a feature of foreign pagan temples.

Verse 19 continues, "Do not bring into the Lord your God's temple the votary offering of a harlot's payment, nor an offering which was exchanged for a dog ..." Here too, the earlier prostitute is seeking to have herself and her profession accepted, while the mention of the dog is picked up next with the repetition of "bite" which follows: "Do not bite into your neighbor's money [taking interest], nor bite into food, nor bite into anything ..." (verse 20).

Then, the harlot's rejected offering is replaced by a required offering: "Should you make a pledge to the Lord your God, do not delay payment, for the Lord your God will expect it of you, lest you incur a sin. Rather, stop your pledging and you will incur no sin ..." (verse 22).

Chapter 25 expounds the law of levirate marriage: "When two brothers live together and one dies leaving no offspring, do not let the widow marry an outsider, but have her brother-in-law take her for wife ... But if he declares, 'I do not want to take her,' then his sister-in-law is to step up to him before the elders, remove his shoe from his foot, spit at him, and respond, 'Thus be it done to a man who will not re-establish his brother's home.'" This ritual is followed by a case involving a totally different married couple: "If two men, a man and a fellow, are wrangling, and one of the wives intervenes to save her husband from his assailant, and if she extends her hand and grabs his private parts, then punish her hand – do not look away" (25:11). Here the pendulum has swung to the opposite extreme, with the wife being overly and unlawfully devoted to her husband, while in the prior levirate case the couple rejected their erstwhile togetherness.

Chapter 25's final statement projects an Israel that is secure on its homeland and being commanded to attack the Amalekites, whom God had condemned to extinction for their surprise attack against the newly-freed Hebrews: "When it comes to pass that the Lord your God rids you of all the enemies around the land which He bequeaths to you, obliterate any remainder of Amalek from under the sky. Don't forget" (25:18).

Chapter 26 swings to finding Israel fully at peace on its fertile soil, and depicts a farmer bringing his First Fruits to "the place that God will have selected to place His name there." The priest accepts the First Fruit offering, and the celebrant responds with a recitation of Israel's history under God's beneficent providence. Then a second recitation is prescribed for a citizen who completes the distribution of his tithes, ending with, "I have done all that you commanded me ... in this land flowing with milk and honey." Aside from the legislative aspects of these two rituals, Moses is returning to his purposeful emboldening of Israel for the wars against Canaan by projecting a bountiful outcome.

Indeed, Moses is reintroduced at this juncture for a new oration, but this time he will be speaking jointly with the nation's elders.

That Israel's elders are now to stand with Moses points to the successful reception of Moses' prior communications. But more to the point, the elders join in this new oration because it sets up a program for the crossing of the Jordan, an event that Moses will not live to see. "On the day that you cross the Jordan erect monumental stones, plaster them, and write on them all the word of this Torah ..." (27:2). Here we have the second time that the Torah refers to itself as being a text – seemingly as an ongoing document – but here to be written on boulders instead of scroll.

Verse 4 adds an attendant ritual, "... thereafter set up these stones on Mount Ebal ... and build there unto the Lord your God a sacrificial altar of whole stones which were not hewn with an ax." Such a plain altar was prescribed in Exodus 20, prior to the elaborate altars required for the future Tabernacle. Thus, we have here another instance of Moses' avoidance of mention or association with the Tabernacle in his Deuteronomy teachings.

The next time that Moses is reintroduced, he is addressing the people together with the priests and Levites. Here too Moses orders a national event which he will not live to attend, the aforementioned blessings and curses for Mount Gerizim and Mount Ebal, with the text here limited to the curses version, concluding with, "Cursed be he who will not uphold the words of this Torah to enact them. And the entire nation shall answer, 'Amen'" (27:26).

But Moses then launches out into his own immediate blessings and curses, using a full 69 verses, of which only fourteen are for the blessing part: "If you obey the Lord your God ... blessed be you in the city and blessed in the field ... blessed at your arrival and blessed at your departure" (28:1). Using the same language in reverse for disobedience: "Cursed be you in the city and cursed in the field ... cursed at your arrival and cursed at your departure."

Verse 58 contains the Torah text's third self-reference, in passing, "... this, if you do not observe all the words of this Torah, which are inscribed in this book." And again in verse 61, "Even all the sicknesses and maladies which are not written in this Torah shall the Lord heap upon you until you expire."

The concluding 69th verse has a surprise: "These are the words of the covenant which the Lord ordered Moses to establish with the Children of Israel while in the land of Moab besides the covenant which he established with them at Horeb." Thus, what initially seemed like wonderful promises versus dire warnings, turns out to be a technical aspect of this new covenant. That is, this 69-verse contract is parallel to the Leviticus chapter-26 text, the 49-verse covenant of Sinai – here called Horeb – which was established forty years earlier. Moses goes on to remind Israel of the salient points of this 40-year experience, but soon enough returns to the covenant and its meaning: "Today you are all in attendance before the Lord your God ... to enter into the covenant and the declamations of the Lord your God, which he sets up with you today. It renders you as His nation and He as your God ..." (29:9).

Chapter 30 depicts the oft-repeated prophecy of Exile and Redemption, first found in the fourth chapter of Deuteronomy.

Chapter 31 begins, "Moses went and spoke the following to all Israel, saying to them, I am today one hundred twenty years old, I cannot stir further, and the Lord has told me not to go beyond this Jordan." The high significance of this address is indicated by the added "to all Israel," meaning to the nation. In this address Moses touches again on every significant idea, theme, and issue that appears in the present book, including a repeat of the victory over the Amorites as evidence of future conquests. The narration then reports: "Moses wrote out this Torah and handed it to the priests, sons of Levi, who carry the Ark of God's Covenant, and to all the elders of Israel." Moses returns to address them, enunciating Torah's last commandment: "At the end of seven years, at the time of the Remission Year during the Festival of Booths, when all Israel come to show themselves before the Lord your God at the place which He will choose, read out this Torah for all Israel to hear...." And here we have the sixth reference of the Torah text to itself.

All at once, God appears as an active participant in the ongoing narrative: "Said the Lord to Moses, 'Your day of death draws near; call to Joshua and stand together in the Tent of Assembly so that I can charge him'" (31:14). Two more Divine appearances will follow, with each reasserting that Moses is going to die. But here God continues, "Now write for yourselves this lyric poem and teach it to the Children of Israel. Have them recite it, so that this lyric poem will serve as my evidence for the Children of Israel." Which poem is meant is not yet known here, but it is to be fully presented in chapter 34, to constitute the longest lyric piece in the Pentateuch:

> Heaven and earth, hear what I say,
> Spread the word like your rain and dew,
> Like storms over meadow and showers on lawns;
> Because it is God's name I proclaim,
> Let us show the reverence that's due:
> The Lord's work is always perfect,
> He is correct in His every way:
> True, unfailing, righteous, and just.
> The holocausts you ask? Not His fault
> But the fault of his children,
> In decadent and corrupt generations.
> Would you blame God, you low fools,
> When He is your father and founder
> Who created and nurtured you?
> Think back to the Beginning,
> Then examine the course of history,
> Ask parents and elders who will tell you:
> When the Lord apportioned the nations,
> When the Lord distinguished the races,
> He did so for the few Israelites,
> Because the Lord wanted His people,
> The Jew was His chosen lot.
>
> He discovered them in the wilderness,
> In the wild howling abyss,
> He befriended them and enlightened them,
> Guarding them like the apple of an eye.
> Like an eagle rousing its brood,
> Hovering gently over its chicks,
> Extending its wing to lift them,
> Then carrying them on its back.
> So God too placed His apart,
> Beyond the reach of any foreign power,
> Transporting them to the heights,
> Feeding them the fruit of the land,

Providing honey and oils amid the rocks,
Milk and cream from cattle and sheep,
With choice cuts of lamb and rams of Bashan,
Golden grain and luscious wine grapes.

But the Israelites grew fat and insolent;
Became opulent, muscular, rebellious;
They abandoned the Lord, demeaned Him;
They pained Him with idols and abominations,
They sacrificed to ghastly divinities
That their patriarchs would not recognize,
And forgot the Lord who gave them life.

God, enraged by His children, groaned:
I will hide My presence from them,
Let's see if they can endure –
These rough youths without manners.
They intimidate Me with false gods,
I will intimidate them with barbarians.
My anger is a fire reaching hell,
Consuming the earth, with its greenery,
And engulfing the steepest mountains.
I shall mobilize terror against them,
Together with the rest of my weaponry:
Hunger, fury, goblins, mad dogs and rattlesnakes,
Death by the sword outside, fear inside,
For boy, girl, infant, and the aged.
I thought: "Damn them, let's erase
Their names from the memory of men …"

Were it not for the ready antisemites,
Lest they claim a victory, saying,
"We win," whereas God lets them.
They plan evils but understand nothing,
For if they were wise they'd ask:
How could one man defeat a thousand,
Or two men trap a population,
Unless their Lord sold them out?

But they do not know our Lord,
Because our enemies are idolators,
Their roots are in Sodom, in the fields
Of Gomorrah growing poison grapes,
For wines like snake's venom.
The Lord has the evidence against them,
To exact a condemnation when the time comes,
And their downfall comes swiftly now,
On the day God seeks justice for His people,
When He sees it powerless and in despair,
Taunted: "Where is the God you trusted,
Who received your sacrifices and libations?
Let Him bestir himself to save you!"

"Here I am, I myself alone,
Am come to slaughter and to heal,
And nothing will stand in my way.
I now raise My hand to Heaven
To swear by My own eternal being,
That I'll not drop the blade of my sword.
Until I take revenge on the enemy;
My arrows will find blood, My sword flesh,
Of the leaders of the pogrom hordes."

The world will cheer God's people,
When He avenges the spilled blood of his servants,
Repaying their enemies with just deserts,
And cleansing His land and His nation.

This poem contains, inter alia, the final reformulation of Deuteronomy's Exile and Redemption prophecy. At its conclusion we are told, "Moses came forth and read out all the words of this lyric poem in the hearing of the Children of Israel, he and Hoshea [Joshua] son of Nun." The Hebrew for Joshua here is Hoshea, not Joshua as Moses had lovingly renamed him in Numbers chapter 13. Joshua's original name Hoshea is used to underscore that, as Moses' leadership is being withdrawn, Joshua is seen as standing on his own authority, as authorized by the Divine, in 31:23.

Verse 24 continues, "Then it was that Moses finished the writing of the words of this Torah on scroll, completely . . ." But this
Torah went on to quote the long lyric in chapter 34, as well as two
more full chapters!

What we seem to have is an avoidance of the Torah concluding with the sort of finality expected in a dramatic epic, or with
the culmination of the plot line expected in a multi-volume narrative. Rather the Torah's conclusion is meant to leave the reader
pondering the expressions of things to come, such as the repeated
prophecies of Exile and Redemption, such as the heady vision of
life in a future land of milk and honey, and by the enactment of a
future legislative system of justice, and by the instructions for the
education of future generations. The text's half-dozen premature
references to its own completion, contributes as well to this understanding of how the Torah draws to a close.

A look to the future, after the final period, is supported further
by the book's last few lines, for example, "Joshua son of Nun was
full of the spirit of wisdom . . . so that the Children of Israel went
on to obey him, doing all that the Lord had commanded Moses.
There never again arose a prophet in Israel such as Moses." Like-
wise, on the death of Moses, "and no man discovered his grave to
this day" (34:6). Thus, we have here three projections to the future.

Even Moses' death does not come as a culminating event that
might have served as a narrative conclusion. First of all, his death
was announced and accepted by Moses as early as the 27th chapter
of the Book of Numbers. Secondly, the sudden appearance of God
Himself in a book devoted to Moses' orations is meant in part to
render Moses' death as a foregone conclusion, since each of the
book's three Divine interventions proclaims the death of Moses.

In addition, Moses conveys an awareness of his looming demise throughout his orations. This he expresses with the thematic
word "today," which appears in Moses' pronouncements some
four dozen times. An early example is, "Today I call on heaven and
earth as witness . . ." (4:26). The last example is, "Take to heart all
the words with which I forewarn you today . . ." (32:46). This final
example is followed by, "God spoke to Moses on this very day, to
say, 'Go up this mountain . . . and die . . .'" (verse 48). We have here
the meaning of Moses' repeated use of "today" in his orations:

that each day is still his living day. He is thereby expressing his urgency to act and speak while he still has a day of life, and in the consciousness that he will soon pass away, as God ordained.

The final phrase in the book reads, "... that which Moses did in the sight of all Israel." Looking at the endings of the other books of the Pentateuch we see that Israel is mentioned again and again. The Book of Exodus concludes, "... in the sight of all the House of Israel, in all their travels." The Book of Leviticus ends, "... the commandments which the Lord gave Moses for the Children of Israel at Mount Sinai." And the Book of Numbers ends, "... the laws the Lord commanded through Moses for the Children of Israel on the plains of Moab, along the Jordan near Jericho." These endings project Israel as the Torah's ultimate subject. And Moses' final pronouncement comes in the form of a benediction for the people and tribes of Israel. While in his earlier speeches Moses castigates them, even characterizing them a stiff-necked rebellious nation, he ends by blessing them and prophesying a glorious future for them in the land beyond the Jordan:

Moses, the man of God, blessed the Children of Israel, before his death, as follows....

Long live Reuben, never die, and may his population multiple.

And for Judah, he said: O Lord, listen to the cries of Judah and bring him home safely. His armies will be victorious when You help him vanquish his foe.

As for Levi, he said: O Lord, grant Your revelations to this devotee, whom You tested in the wilderness and admonished over stormy waters. He can brush aside a father and mother, be a stranger to his brothers, even disown his own children, in order to obey Your commandments and to keep Your covenant. He can teach righteousness to Jacob, teach Torah to Israel. He is the one to place frankincense before You and a burnt offering on Your altar. O Lord, bless his fighters, granting success to their every maneuver, smashing the underbelly of the enemy so he can never rise again.

For Benjamin he proclaimed: God loves him, God is with him always, hovering over him all day long and resting between his peaks.

As for Joseph, he declared: May the Lord bless his land with the riches of heaven's dew and the flow of underground rivers. With the riches of sun-ripe grain and the riches of succulent nightshades, from the tops of ancient mountains to the terraces of timeless hills, with the bounty of a fertile land. All this, because he finds favor with He Who Descended To The Thornbush. May all this crown the head of Joseph, a prince among his brothers. As handsome as a thoroughbred steer, like a stag with twin antlers with which he butts away to land's end – these antlers representing the armies of Ephraim and the divisions of Menashe.

To Zebulun he said: Enjoy the success of your ventures Zebulun, while Issachar tends the home office. Now call your agents back to a mountain retreat to render the thanksgiving offering, for they amassed profits from overseas, gathering the treasures of distant shores.

For Gad he said: Blessed be He who gives Gad his space, where he lives lion-like, tearing at head and shoulders. He took first choice in a land of fabled wealth, having won the approval of the nation's leaders, and doing what is right and just before God and Israel.

For Dan he said: Dan too is like a young lion, romping through the Bashan.

For Naphtali he said: A happy man is Naphtali, in the possession of the lakes down South.

And for Asher he said: Asher is like a lucky boy, the delight of his brothers, wading in rich deposits of oil, and with iron and copper in the foothills. Asher never has a bad day.

O Righteous People, there is none like the Lord, who comes riding the heavens like a spirited bronco to rescue you. He is the overlord of the forces of creation, and the underpinning of the universe's base. He can repel the challengers who confront you, letting you merely give chase, in order to settle Israel securely – alone around Jacob's water source – in a land of wheat and wine, under a sky dripping with dew.

O Fortunate Israel, there is none like you, a nation protected by God's proud sword and shield, so that your foes shrink before you, while you trample their embankments.

A Son Remembers

My father MORDECAI LICHTENSTEIN
Laid to rest 1997 in Jerusalem.

My mother PESSA LEA (KINEK) LICHTENSTEIN
Laid to rest 1988 in Baltimore.

My grandfather SHMUEL GRONEM LICHTENSTEIN
Laid to rest 1947 on Mount Olives.